GOOD

TIDINGS OF

GREAT JOY

Good Tidings of Great Joy, *by Walter Rane. Used by permission.*

GOOD
TIDINGS OF
GREAT JOY

AN ADVENT CELEBRATION
OF THE SAVIOR'S BIRTH

ERIC D. HUNTSMAN

DESERET
BOOK

Salt Lake City, Utah

uxori amatae filiisque carissimis

To my beloved wife,
Elaine, a woman of Christ
whose devotion to family and the gospel
makes our house a home overflowing with love and the Spirit,
especially at Christmas

To my dearest children,
Rachel and Samuel, precious souls
whose love of Jesus and excitement each year
fill our lives and hearts with joy,
making every Christmas magical

Library of Congress Cataloging-in-Publication Data
Huntsman, Eric D., 1965– author.
    Good tidings of great joy : an Advent celebration of the Savior's birth / Eric D. Huntsman.
        pages cm
    Includes bibliographical references and index.
    ISBN 978-1-60641-659-4 (hardbound : alk. paper)
    1. Jesus Christ—Nativity.   2. Advent.   3. Christmas.   I. Title.
    BT315.3.H86 2011
    263'.91—dc23
                                                                                    2011013304

Printed in Mexico
R. R. Donnelley, Reynosa, Mexico

10   9   8   7   6   5   4   3   2   1

CONTENTS

PREFACE

Good Tidings of Great Joy is a celebration, an exploration of the scriptural stories surrounding our Savior's birth, augmented by art, photographs of Holy Land sites, music, reflections, and short discussions of detailed issues. Organized around the good tidings of the birth of Jesus Christ in the accounts of Matthew and Luke, it culminates with the glad tidings found in Book of Mormon prophecies, which emphasize that the coming of Jesus was important because of what he would do—suffering, dying, and rising again for us all. Thus as a companion volume to *God So Loved the World,* my earlier treatment of the Easter season, this scriptural celebration serves as the first part of our journey exploring the greatest story ever told.

Our celebration begins with a full introduction that briefly traces the history of Christmas, outlines the importance of family and church celebrations, and reflects upon the experience my family and I have had in rediscovering the true meaning of Christmas, particularly by focusing on the scriptural stories that serve as a foundation for our yearly commemoration of the Savior's birth. Our scriptural journey then proceeds with chapters exploring Matthew and Luke's detail-rich Infancy Narratives. These chapters examine familiar stories—such as those of Joseph, Zacharias, Elisabeth, Mary, the birth of John the Baptist, the miraculous birth of Jesus Christ, the adoration of the shepherds, the visit of the Magi, and others—with the added insight of biblical scholarship, the testimony of Restoration scripture and latter-day authorities, and personal experiences. After this, the final chapter presents further glad tidings in the form of a Book of Mormon Christmas, adding the stories of Nephi, King Benjamin, Alma, Samuel the Lamanite, and Nephi the son of Nephi to the Bible's testimonies. Woven between these chapters are reflections on the traditional Advent themes of Hope, Love, Joy, and Peace, to which I have added a fifth, Salvation.

The conclusion of our celebration considers how we can remember Christmas throughout the year. Beginning with Christmas Day, we can continue to nurture the spirit of Christmas during the year by keeping the Savior foremost in our minds, hearts, and actions. We can do this particularly by remembering how the Babe of Bethlehem became the Man of the Gospels, whose life and ministry culminated in the glad tidings of salvation that came through his atoning sacrifice and joyous Resurrection.

Three appendices supplement this celebration of Christmas. The first, "The Infancy Narratives and the Christmas Story," contains a discussion of some of the scholarly background behind the main chapters of the book. It reviews important historical, literary, and theological components of the Infancy Narratives. The second, "Preparing for Christmas," is a family resource guide consisting of a list of scriptures, carols, and stories that I have prepared for every day of December. The third, "Christmas with Autism," is a personal essay about my family's experience celebrating Christmas with a special-needs child, sharing the joy we have had in using this happiest of holidays as a teaching opportunity that has blessed our son's life—and ours.

Hopefully this book can deepen or add to your own celebration of Christmas, leavening it with a focus on the scriptural accounts of the stories surrounding our Savior's birth. Traditionally, some Christians begin preparing to celebrate Christmas four weeks before the holiday through the observance of the Advent season. While this is not a widespread Latter-day Saint practice, many of us at least read from the Christmas story on Christmas Eve, usually the familiar story from Luke 2:1–14. I suggest that in the four weeks leading up to Christmas some may want to study one chapter a week from Matthew 1–2 and Luke 1–2, possibly using the discussions in the chapters of this book as a guide. Perhaps the fifth and final chapter about the Book of Mormon's contribution to the story can be read after Christmas, helping connect your celebration of the Savior's birth with the final days of his life.

My wish is that this book may make your own observance of Christmas more meaningful by keeping Christ and the salvation he offers central to the entire Christmas season—and the entire year. As I observed in *God So Loved the World,* the stories of Christmas and Easter are intricately connected to one another. Both celebrate the glad tidings that God so loved the world that he sent his Son—as a gift at his birth, a sacrifice at his death, and a source of hope at his Resurrection.

ACKNOWLEDGMENTS

I have dedicated this book to my wife and children. Each year I have the opportunity to experience Christmas with my family, and Rachel and Samuel inspire Elaine and me to share our faith in Jesus with them even as they add to our delight in the season.

I must also acknowledge my mother, Marilyn Halversen Huntsman. Like most parents, she and Dad provided me with wonderful Christmas traditions and memories. But in addition, by providing me workspace in her home while I was on academic leave in 2010, Mother contributed in a very direct way to the writing of both this book and *God So Loved the World*, my earlier treatment of the Easter season.

I am thankful to Alan Farnes, Eric Schetselaar, and especially my assistant, Joshua Matson, for reading the manuscript, making corrections, and checking sources. In particular, I owe a great debt of gratitude to my friend and colleague Kelly Ogden, who carefully reviewed the entire manuscript and made helpful suggestions. I also express appreciation to Dennis Largey, chair of Ancient Scripture at Brigham Young University, and to David Seely of the Religious Study Center for their support of this project.

Chad Emmett, Kent Jackson, and Kerry Muhlestein generously shared their photographs of the Holy Land, and Rita Wright once again served as a helpful consultant on much of the fine art that appears in this volume.

I am grateful to my friend George Durrant, who taught me how to better tell a story, bear testimony, and touch a heart.

Music is a central part of the celebration of Christmas, and it accordingly plays an important role in this book. Andrew Unsworth and Ryan Murphy were helpful in discussing with me some of the musical selections that appear here. While not directly connected to this work, other important musical and personal inspirations to me include Mack Wilberg, Craig Jessop, and Richard Elliott.

As always, my final thanks is to Almighty God, as well as to his Son, Jesus Christ, whose birth, life, sacrifice, and Resurrection give my life—and future eternities—meaning.

*May You Have a Wonderful
Christmas Season!*

It is our hope that this book will
provide years of insights, knowledge,
and traditions to help you enhance the
spirituality of your Christmas
observance.

This year we have specifically used it
as a resource for the Sundays of
Advent, listing the themes and pages on
your box notes- We hope it brings some
depth and help as you prepare your
devotional times. The advent is also
explained on pgs 16-17.

There is also an interesting Resource
Guide in Appendix 2.

Merry Christmas!

We Love You

Introduction
CELEBRATING CHRISTMAS

This is a glorious time of the year, simple in origin, deep in meaning, beautiful in tradition and custom, rich in memories, and charitable in spirit. It has an attraction to which our hearts are readily drawn. This joyful season brings to each of us a measure of happiness that corresponds to the degree in which we have turned our mind, feelings, and actions, to the spirit of Christmas.

—President Thomas S. Monson

As noted by President Monson, the Christmas season is a glorious, joyful time of the year.[1] A number of factors combine to make the traditions, music, customs, decorations, feelings, and even foods of Christmastime so special to us. These may include happy memories from our childhood and warm, loving feelings from our present. The celebration of Christmas that creates these feelings in us developed over the centuries into what it has become today, when family and religious traditions play such an important role in this most happy of holidays. Yet above all, the story of that first Christmas is what evokes the true spirit of Christmas most in our hearts. It is a story that we know primarily from the opening chapters of Matthew and Luke, but we also know it from music, art, and stories from elsewhere in the scriptures.

How we appreciate these stories plays a vital role in helping us rediscover the true meaning of Christmas. Better understanding them leads us to turn more fully to our Savior and thereby find the spirit of this holy season. Nevertheless, the stories of our Savior's birth are intricately tied to the stories of his saving death and subsequent victory over the grave. As President Hinckley noted in his December 2000 Christmas message, "There would be no Christmas if there had not been Easter. The babe Jesus of Bethlehem would be but another baby without the redeeming Christ of Gethsemane and Calvary, and the triumphant fact of the Resurrection."[2] Still, the joyous celebration of Easter morning each year comes with the serious realization that Jesus Christ's triumphant victory over sin, suffering, and death came at a terrible and painful cost, an understanding which tempers our joy as we soberly reflect upon the events that preceded the empty tomb.

Like Temple Square, Manger Square in Bethlehem is brightly decorated with lights for the Christmas holiday.

During the Christmas season the festive lights of Temple Square in Salt Lake City convey the joy of Jesus' birth. Courtesy of Shutterstock. Used by permission.

Perhaps this sober realization at Easter time helps account for some of our enthusiasm for Christmas, when our commemoration of the Savior's birth generally does not carry the seriousness of Good Friday. Still, as we celebrate the Christmas story each year, we should remember that it is part of a much larger story: that God so loved the world that he sent his Son, "as a gift at his birth" to be sure, but also as "a sacrifice at his death, and as a source of hope at his Resurrection."[3]

A Brief History of Christmas

Of course, today cultural and even commercial factors play major roles in making Christmas perhaps the most popular Christian holiday, both for believers and also for those who do not necessarily share our faith in Jesus Christ. Thus, while Easter remains in theological terms the more important holiday, Christmas is clearly the most popular both in practice and sentiment. Surprisingly, however, the scriptures do not seem to indicate that the earliest New Testament Christians celebrated the birth of Jesus in any formal way. Most of the first Christians were also Jews, and even after the law of Moses was fulfilled, they seem to have continued to observe some of the Mosaic festivals such as Pentecost (see Acts 2:1) and Passover (see Acts 12:4, where the KJV renders it as "Easter"). But for these Jewish Christians, and for the Gentiles who were subsequently brought into the Christian movement, the emphasis in the New Testament–era church seems to have been on what we today call Easter and the events surrounding it. In other words, they focused on the proclamation of the "good news" (Greek, *euangellion*) that Jesus had suffered, died, and rose again for us. The speeches of Peter and Paul as preserved in Acts, the epistles of these two Apostles, and the writings of others in the New Testament focus on the Atonement of Jesus Christ—both the redemption and the Resurrection that he accomplished on our behalf. The Gospel of Mark—which was probably composed in the last half of the first century and is considered the first of the New Testament Gospels—also began not with Jesus' birth but with the opening of his Galilean ministry, and then progressed toward the end of his life, ultimately focusing on his last week.

Nevertheless, the earliest New Testament letters, written possibly before any of the Gospels, contain brief but important references to two vital aspects of the first Christmas story. For instance, in Paul's letter to the Galatians, which is thought to have been written either circa A.D. 49 or 57, he describes how God "sent forth his Son, made of a woman" (Galatians 4:4), thus giving us the earliest, though oblique, Christian reference to Mary's giving birth to Jesus. In A.D. 57 or 58, when Paul addressed Christians living in Rome, he wrote "concerning [God's] Son Jesus Christ our Lord, which was made of the seed of David according to the flesh" (Romans 1:3), revealing that the first Christians knew that Jesus was indeed the promised king of the house and lineage of David.

Matthew and then Luke, both perhaps written in the decade beginning A.D. 70, were the first—and the only—New Testament authors to take these basic facts and weave them together with a number of other important details about Jesus' origins into a full story. Their accounts of the divine

The Nativity, *by Giotto di Bondone, detail.*

conception and miraculous birth of Jesus, which biblical scholars usually refer to as Infancy Narratives, were a significant addition to the genre of Gospel writing that Mark pioneered. Matthew and Luke's Infancy Narratives, which at their beginnings respond to the early Christians' desire to know more about *who* Jesus actually was, also underscore and emphasize *what* Jesus was able to accomplish at the end of the Gospels (see Appendix 1: The Infancy Narratives and the Christmas Story). We are grateful that the beautiful stories that Matthew and Luke preserved serve as the heart of the Christmas that we now celebrate.

While the Infancy Narratives began to serve an important theological role as soon as they were composed, they do not seem to have initially sparked any formal celebrations of Jesus' birth. Still, inspired by stories from the Infancy Narratives, Christians in the second century began to search the Old Testament for allusions to Jesus' coming, following Matthew's Gospel, which drew parallels between Old Testament prophecies and their fulfillment in Christ's life. What these second-century Christians found added symbolic elements to the story of the Nativity, including a greater role for the star at Jesus' birth and the presence of various animals and even kings at the Nativity. Though not included in the Bible, these additions have become a part of our traditional picture of Christmas as depicted in art and music.[4]

Not until the third century did some Christians begin to consider celebrating Christ's birth as a holiday. Even then, some Christian leaders and thinkers at the time, such as Origen (circa A.D. 185–254), resisted the idea because celebrating birthdays was a particularly pagan practice.[5] As Christianity continued to spread, it did so in a Roman world, which celebrated not only birthdays but also a variety of festivals commemorating important events in the lives of leaders and religious figures. Accordingly, Christians became attracted to the idea of celebrating a festival of their own that could stress essential elements of their own faith. While Luke's account suggests that Jesus was born in a season when shepherds would have been in their fields (see Luke 2:8), fourth-century Christians, for a variety of reasons, eventually settled on a date near the winter solstice, which in the ancient Roman calendar fell on December 25. Because that date was a time when many religious traditions and cultures held midwinter festivals, Christians came to find that celebrating Christ's birth instead became a good way to focus on something that reinforced their own faith.[6]

Especially as Christianity spread to northern Europe, the midwinter observance of Christmas as a celebration of joy, light, and life intensified as Christian leaders used the

While Christmas lights probably had their origins in the midwinter festivals of Europe, today the practice has spread around the world, even to tropical areas such as Hawaii.

Courtesy of Kerry Muhlestein.

Today Bethlehem is the scene of many festive preparations for Christmas, such as this parade of local Christians on Christmas Eve Day.

story of Jesus' birth to replace earlier pagan customs in that often darker and colder clime. Yule logs, bonfires, and other means of lighting the cold darkness became fixed features of Christmas.[7] While the symbolism of overcoming darkness with warmth and light continues in the northern hemisphere, the tradition of Christmas lights has spread throughout the world, with lights as a feature of Christmas today even in Australia, South America, South Africa, and the Pacific islands.

Celebrating Christmas grew throughout the Middle Ages, becoming not only an important religious feast but also an important and needed break from the rigors of daily life. Only with the Reformation did observing Christmas suffer a setback, as some scrupulous Protestants, including the Puritans in England and the newly settled North American colonies, felt that Christmas was unbiblical and saw it as too Catholic.[8] Nevertheless, while a few Christian groups today still resist celebrating Christmas, for the most part, Christians have come to not only accept but also rejoice in the Christmas season. In the nineteenth century, Christmas experienced a resurgence as a popular festival, particularly in Victorian England and then later in America, with a wonderful focus on children and families.[9] This development was matched perhaps unfortunately by a growing commercial emphasis, but the positive result of all these factors was that the celebration of Christmas has spread beyond just believers. Now, throughout the world, even non-Christians are aware of the basic stories of Jesus' birth and can enjoy a measure of Christmas joy.[10]

How Christmas Came to Be on December 25

Modern revelation seems to suggest that Jesus was born on April 6 (see D&C 20:1), a proposition that has been widely supported and explained in LDS teaching since.[11] A spring date certainly accords better with the Lucan image of shepherds abiding in the fields, but it also prompts Latter-day Saints to wonder how December 25 became the standard date for Christmas.

Because the Gospels do not give an exact date for Jesus' birth, and because early Christians most likely did not celebrate Christmas, later believers were left to guess at a probable date. Perhaps the earliest assumption was January 6, a date associated with both the visit of the Wise Men and Jesus' later baptism. Giving credence to this date was the association of Jesus' "new birth" at the beginning of his ministry (Mark 1:11, when God proclaimed Jesus to be his Son after he was baptized) replacing his birth as Mary's baby (Luke 2:7). January 6 was also initially popular with some Egyptian Christians because the Osiris myth—which contains symbolic echoes of Christ's life since Osiris was reputed to have risen again after dying—became associated with new year celebrations there.

However, March 25 soon became a more popular date for Jesus' birth because the spring equinox in the Roman calendar fell on that day. Some early Christian writers connected the beginning of spring with the creation of light and of the world, suggesting that it was a fitting day for Jesus, the True Light, to have come into the world. Later, some also suggested that March 25 had been the day of his saving death, thus linking the day when he came into the world with the day when the world was redeemed. One writer, Sextus Julius Africanus (circa A.D. 160–240), connected the Roman spring equinox not to the day of Jesus' birth but rather to the day of his conception. Significantly, this assumption would place Jesus' birth nine months later on December 25, the winter solstice according to the original Roman calendar.

December 25 became particularly important in the third and early fourth centuries when a series of emperors—including Elagabalus, Aurelian, and eventually Constantine—made sun worship a central tenet of Roman belief. This was because the birthdays of *Sol Invictus*, "the Unconquered Sun," and yet another Roman god, Mithras, both fell on the winter solstice. Later, when Christians asserted that Jesus was the true source of light and the actual "Sun of righteousness" (Malachi 4:2), they may have tried to displace such Roman solar deities by converting those holidays to Jesus' birthday. This date did not become official, however, until the Chronograph of 354, in which the church at Rome established December 25 as the date of Jesus' birth. By the end of the fourth century most major Christian churches had accepted this date as well. Because some of the Eastern Orthodox churches continue to use the older Julian calendar, their celebration falls on what our Gregorian calendar calls January 7.

Because December 25 also fell near other Roman festivals, such as the gift-giving holiday known as Saturnalia, observing Christmas on this date allowed Christians to celebrate much as their neighbors did. As Christianity spread into northern Europe, the winter date of Christmas also allowed it to gradually displace other midwinter festivals.[12] Because of this history, commemorating the birth of Jesus on December 25 allows us to celebrate with most of the Christian world and enjoy many of the seasonal traditions that have become part of Christmas through the centuries.

FAMILY AND CHURCH CELEBRATIONS OF CHRISTMAS

For most Latter-day Saints, celebrating Christmas is, as it is for other Christians, primarily a family affair. Most of us work to make our home a happy place and the season a magical and exciting time. Those living far away from family often make considerable efforts to "be home for Christmas." Exchanging gifts with loved ones cements bonds of love and appreciation. As the season progresses, a welcome break in the routine of school and work crescendos beyond simple relief from responsibility to a wonderful sense of festivity. Still, for those committed to "putting Christ back in Christmas" the celebration becomes, above all, an opportunity to commemorate the love of God—that the Father loved us so much that he sent his Son into the world and that the great Jehovah deigned to become the Babe of Bethlehem. For believers it becomes primarily a joyous recognition of our Newborn King, reminding us that as he came in humility the first time, he will come in great glory the second.

In establishing family traditions for Christmas—either traditions that are religious or those that are purely fun—new couples tend to follow a pattern of borrowing and adapting the traditions of each spouse's family and often picking up new traditions along the way. When Elaine and I married, we split our first Christmas between our two families, spending the holiday with my parents in Tennessee and then celebrating all over again with Elaine's parents in New Jersey a few days later. Yet of all the wonderful Christmases we have had together, perhaps my favorite was our second Christmas. In our small, first house after we had taken a job in Utah, we faced the prospect of Christmas without any of our immediate families. But as we spent that Christmas Eve and Christmas morning alone in our new home, we began building traditions of our own, and the recollection of that special Christmas remains one of the warmest in my memory.

Like other couples, we began building our Christmas tradition by following some of our own families' traditions. These included attending a matinee performance of Tchaikovsky's *The Nutcracker* with extended family, having an early dinner out afterward, heading home for a late Christmas Eve snack beside our Christmas tree, lining our front yard with luminarias, getting up at an unreasonable hour on Christmas morning, and preparing particular kinds of foods for Christmas dinner. But some of the customs we established were new to both of us, particularly those that help commemorate the birth of our Savior. For instance, with our first tree we also purchased our first Christmas crèche, a Nativity set with all of the familiar figures and accessories. A year or two later, an aunt gave us a booklet containing scriptures, carols, and Christmas stories for each day in December. We began the practice of using it each year for a Christmas devotional every evening before family prayer (see Appendix 2: Preparing for Christmas: A Family Resource Guide).

Of course, when our daughter, Rachel, was born and then later when our son, Samuel, joined our family, a new level of magic and excitement was added to our family celebration of Christmas. Holiday cartoons and TV shows from my youth reappeared, and Santa Claus regained his earlier prominence. In fact, as LDS storyteller George Durrant has written, "This time [Santa] was bigger and better than

Courtesy of Eric Huntsman.

Many families try to keep the focus of the holiday on the birth of Jesus by setting up a Nativity scene, or crèche, as part of their Christmas decorations.

he had been before. This time he wouldn't be someone to get things from but instead he would be someone to give things through."[13] My sister gave us an Advent calendar modeled after one that she and I had enjoyed as children so that my children could have the same thrill of opening a pocket on the calendar every day to reveal either a felt figure for the Nativity scene or a decoration for the Christmas tree that are featured on the calendar.

The responsibilities of parenthood included a growing sense that Christmas should be, first and foremost, a powerful opportunity to teach our children about Jesus. With Rachel, accomplishing that goal was fairly conventional. We used family home evening lessons and our daily Christmas devotionals to talk about the symbolism of our decorations and the true meaning of the holiday.[14] But because Samuel has challenges associated with his autism, helping him understand and enjoy the holiday involved new ways of thinking and often considerable adaptation (see Appendix 3: Christmas with Autism). Nevertheless, we knew that for both of our children, Christmas presented us with an obligation to teach them not just about Jesus' birth but also about his saving mission. I was grateful that we had the Church to reinforce what we were trying to do at home.

While The Church of Jesus Christ of Latter-day Saints is not as formal in observing Christmas as some other traditions, which hold midnight mass or other services on Christmas Eve, some of our important Christmas celebrations take place among our Church family. For instance, because my mother was the perpetual choir director in every ward and stake we lived in, the members of our family always participated in every aspect of our ward Christmas program. Attending the ward Christmas party and the special Christmas sacrament meeting with its music, scripture readings, and talks remain vital parts of our holiday experience.

In addition, the Church holds events on a general level that members throughout the world can enjoy—if not in person, then through broadcasts and audio and video recordings. For instance, Temple Square in downtown Salt Lake City and Church visitors' centers in other locations are wonderfully decorated with lights and Nativity scenes. The annual First Presidency Devotional, which originated as a devotional held in the Salt Lake Tabernacle for Church employees, has become a Churchwide meeting held in the Conference Center and broadcast by satellite and the Internet throughout the world, thereby becoming a worldwide celebration of the birth of the Savior.[15] Featuring always-inspiring and frequently tender addresses by the First Presidency and music from the Mormon Tabernacle Choir, this devotional has become an event that signals the start of the LDS Christmas season. Likewise, the annual Christmas concert of the Mormon Tabernacle Choir—attended by more than 80,000 annually in the Conference Center and rebroadcast nationally by PBS the following year—has become a Christmas staple not just for members of the Church but for others as well.

Courtesy of Eric Huntsman.

Courtesy of Eric Huntsman.

Top: Decorating the Christmas tree is a favorite tradition of children of all ages, including Rachel and Samuel in this picture from 2008. Bottom: Jokingly called "Little Temple Square" by neighbors, our home is festively lit for Christmas.

The annual First Presidency Devotional, featuring messages from the members of the LDS First Presidency and music by the Mormon Tabernacle Choir and Orchestra at Temple Square, has become a worldwide celebration of Christmas.

REDISCOVERING THE TRUE MEANING OF CHRISTMAS

Even when our family and Church celebrations of Christmas amply focus on the Savior and his birth, it is still sometimes possible to get so caught up in traditions and activities that these foundational stories are eclipsed. I first became aware of this when, in 2000, the calendar caused us to modify some of our usual Christmas traditions. That year Christmas Eve fell on a Sunday. Wanting to keep the Sabbath holy, we needed to do things differently. We attended *The Nutcracker* with our extended family and had our early supper at the traditional hamburger joint a day early. I made the luminarias on Saturday—folding the bags, filling them with sand, placing the candles—while Elaine finished much of the baking and cooking early. On the day of Christmas Eve that year there wouldn't be any frantic last-minute shopping! Most important, we attended church that day with our ward family, just hours before our own family gathered at home to usher in Christmas. Our ward made an extra effort to prepare a special sacrament meeting program. The nearness of Christmas that year made it feel different and even more spiritual than usual.

Perhaps the most striking thing about that Christmas Eve was arriving home after sacrament meeting with the entire afternoon free to spend all my time with my family, listening to beautiful music and enjoying the scents, tastes, and feelings of Christmas. I had more time than usual with the scriptures, studying the Infancy Narratives with more attention than I had in other years, reading them over and over again. The well-known first half of Luke 2 had been something we had either read together or watched as a video dramatization each year, but this was the first time I had focused on *all* the scriptural stories of the Savior's birth. That evening our usual Christmas Eve traditions had a different—and holier—feel.

That experience has become an important spiritual point of reference for me, especially as my professional interests in subsequent years moved toward biblical studies. In the process I discovered many wonderful resources that provide insights into the Christmas story through the careful analysis of the surrounding history, languages, and the texts themselves.[16] Yet while I continue to value combining faith and scholarship, sometimes I find this approach less satisfying when studying the Infancy Narratives. I still enjoy learning new details and seeing familiar passages in fresh ways, and some faithful scholarship helps reinforce my faith.[17] But at times some scholarship focuses almost single-mindedly on the differences between Matthew's and Luke's accounts, emphasizing the seeming contradictions more than considering the fundamental points they share. In those instances scholarship by itself does little to reinforce my own conviction that the basic story is true—and not just true but

Christmas in Art

Courtesy of Bridgeman Art Library. Used by permission.

These details from the Sarcophagus of the Nativity, dating to the fourth century and depicting both Jesus in a manger and the visit of the Three Magi, are among the earliest pieces of Christmas art.

The earliest depictions of the Christmas story in art date to the fourth century, about the time that the church in Rome settled on December 25 as the date of Christ's birth and made that day a religious feast. The image of the baby Jesus wrapped and lying in a manger began to be depicted on Christian sarcophagi, and Mary, Joseph, and the Wise Men in similar fashion somewhat later. Early paintings of such scenes began to appear in catacombs in Rome (see "The Christmas Crèche," Chapter 3). In subsequent centuries, artistic depictions of the Nativity became common in a number of media, particularly in the Middle Ages and Renaissance when many of our commonly recognized Christmas images became set.[18] Indeed, each of the episodes of the Christmas story—such as the Annunciation to Mary, the Nativity, the Adoration of the Shepherds, the Adoration of the Magi, and the Presentation in the Temple—have become important cycles of art.

Christmas has continued to inspire artists, small and great, through the centuries, as seen in the well-known works of James Tissot, Carl Bloch, and now many Latter-day Saint artists whose works continue to inspire viewers, reminding them of the good tidings of the Savior's birth. The art of these and others appears throughout this book to inspire you and help you imagine the stories that the scriptures tell.

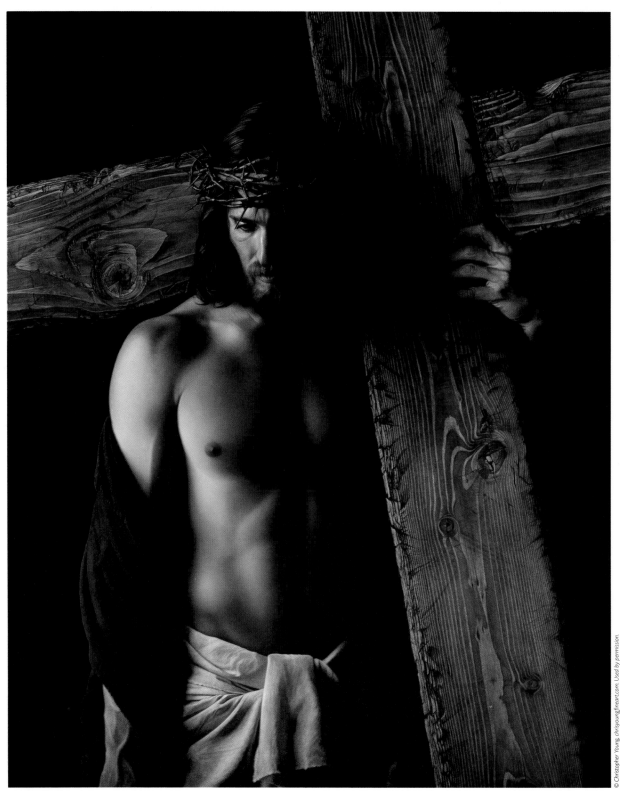

Man of Sorrows, *by Christopher Young.*

vital.[19] As a result, when my studies leave me feeling deflated or feeling somehow that some of the joy in the Christmas stories has been lost, I shut my commentaries and remember the spirit I felt reading just the scriptures that special Sunday Christmas Eve afternoon.

The first time I taught a Book of Mormon class at Brigham Young University, I found yet another resource to serve as a corrective to an occasionally sagging Christmas spirit. As I prepared my syllabus for fall semester, I realized that the class would meet once more than usual. With room for another lecture, I decided to plan a lesson called "A Book of Mormon Christmas" for our final meeting. When the time arrived to prepare that lecture, I combed the Book of Mormon prophecies of Jesus' arrival and birth. What I found was that the Book of Mormon supported those vital parts of the Christmas story where Matthew and Luke agreed most clearly. Further, Book of Mormon prophecies gave me a sharper lens to see how the coming of Jesus connected intricately to the ultimate part of his mission at the end of his mortal life—the good tidings of Jesus' birth in the New Testament complemented by the glad tidings in the Book of Mormon explaining "why He came into the world."[20]

Connecting the beginning of the story with its end has served as the impetus of this book. Having had the opportunity to study and share the importance of the events

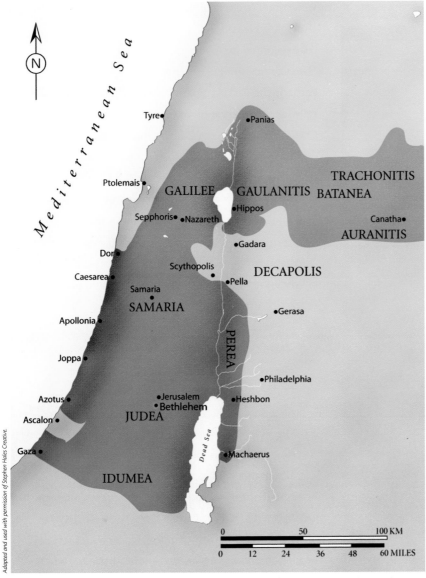

Adapted and used with permission of Stephen Hales Creative.

At the time of Jesus' birth, the Holy Land was ruled by Herod the Great, a client ruler closely allied with the Roman Empire. The annunciation to Mary took place in Nazareth, located in the northern region of Galilee. The accounts of Matthew and Luke agree that Jesus was born in Bethlehem, the original city of David, just south of Jerusalem in Judea.

The Development of Christmas Music

An integral part of the celebration of Christmas today is listening to or singing seasonal music, especially Christmas carols. The word *carol* seems to have its origin in the Greek *choros,* which in antiquity was as much a dance as it was a song. It came into English through the Old French *carole,* which originally referred to a popular dance accompanied by singers, and since then carols have come to refer to any festive songs associated with a major holiday, particularly for those sung at Christmastime. To a certain extent the Christmas carol was

anticipated by the religious songs (or canticles) that Luke recorded for figures in his Infancy Narratives (see "The Canticles in Luke," Chapter 2: Promised Savior). Perhaps the earliest poems or songs written specifically for the celebration of Christmas came from early Christian writers in the fourth century A.D.[21]

Surviving examples of such early Christmas hymns come from Ephrem the Syrian (circa A.D. 306–373), who wrote a collection of hymns about the Nativity in Syriac, a language related to Hebrew and Aramaic, and from Aurelius Prudentius Clemens (circa A.D. 348–405), who wrote a *Hymn for Christmas* in Latin. Much of Prudentius' hymn, such as the part quoted here, has echoes in current carols:

> It was upon this very day
> That God put on our mortal clay.
> The noble Virgin's time is near,
> And—joy to the world!—her Child is here. . . .
> All nature exults! And the least of us,
> The simplest herdsman prays, and his sheep
> And cattle adore the baby, asleep
> In the rude cradle. . . .[22]

Also written by Prudentius was the text *Corde natus ex parentis* ("Of the Father's Love Begotten"). Other Christmas hymns from the fourth century include *Jesus refulsit omnium* ("Jesus, Light of All the Nations") by Hilary of Poitiers (circa A.D. 315–368) and *Veni redemptor gentium* ("Come, Redeemer of the Nations")

Singing Angels, by Van Eyck.

by Ambrose of Milan (circa A.D. 340–397). No kind of musical notation is preserved for any of these earliest hymns, and the earliest known "carols" in the usual sense are probably those of medieval Latin plainchants, which were unaccompanied single-melody songs that would have been used during the extended feast of Christmastide (which we know as the "Twelve Days of Christmas" from December 25 through Epiphany on January 6). Regional variations eventually produced the antecedents of more familiar forms in fifteenth-century English carols and French *noëls*.

With the Reformation, the rise of Lutheranism was accompanied by the development of the German Christmas chorale and other great religious music for the season by important figures such as Michael Praetorius (1571–1621), Johann Sebastian Bach (1685–1750), and German-born George Frideric Handel (1685–1759). Protestantism in other areas of Europe, however, was not as friendly to either the celebration of Christmas or to Christmas music. Nevertheless, after a decline and sometimes outright suppression of Christmas music in England during the seventeenth century, the tradition of congregational singing early in the eighteenth and nineteenth centuries, and then especially the emphasis on Christmas in the Victorian era led to a rich outpouring of music in England that was paralleled in America.[23]

While the format of this book does not allow an extensive survey of Christmas music, each chapter begins with a suggestion for a great Christmas masterwork and continues with periodic musical reflections on carols where the texts or sometimes the music itself supports the exposition of the Infancy Narratives. Even more familiar and well-loved carols are included in Appendix 2: Preparing for Christmas: A Family Resource Guide.

leading up to Easter in another book,[24] I have felt a great desire to share the experience I have had in learning how to better celebrate Christmas, making it more meaningful by focusing on the scriptural stories surrounding the Savior's birth, and discovering how they influence so much of our music, art, traditions, and celebrations. Above all, I have found that truly celebrating Christmas involves much more—seeing how the good tidings of Jesus' birth are ultimately about something else, the good news of his promised gift, salvation. ❖

CELEBRATING ADVENT

As part of preparing for Christmas, Christians from some backgrounds observe a custom called Advent. This observance takes its name from the Latin *adventus*, which means "coming" or "appearance." As such, Advent is a way that some choose to celebrate the coming of Jesus into the world at his birth, to focus on his presence in their lives now, and to look forward to his glorious return in the future. Whether gathered in church or at home, those who observe Advent today use the Sundays leading up to Christmas to prepare themselves through scriptures, music, and other traditions. While Advent is

The lit candles of the Huntsman family Advent wreath add to the beauty of their Christmas tree's lights on Christmas Eve.

not a regular part of Latter-day Saint practice, individual families, such as ours, have found that incorporating some aspects of it into their own traditions at home can be a wonderful way to keep the Christmas season Christ-centered.

Advent was originally a solemn, preparatory period before newly converted Christians were baptized on January 6. That day was selected for such baptisms because it was the day, particularly in the East, that commemorated Jesus' own baptism. Perhaps because of that date's proximity to Christmas, Pope Gregory the Great (A.D. 590–604) later established Advent as a period of preparation anticipating the Feast of the Nativity, a period that he set as beginning on the fourth Sunday before Christmas. While the Reformation led some later Protestants to stop observing Advent, Martin Luther, who loved the Christmas season, felt that it was still a useful way to teach children and families about the importance of the coming of the Babe of Bethlehem. As a result, Advent continued to be particularly important in Germany, from whence many of its customs have spread.[1]

Perhaps the best-known Advent custom is the lighting of candles in an Advent wreath, a simple or decorated evergreen wreath with four candles placed in the circle and sometimes a single white candle in the center. In his First Presidency Christmas Devotional address in 2008, President Dieter F. Uchtdorf remembered this custom from his own childhood: "When I was very young and living in East Germany, Christmas in our family began four weeks before Christmas Eve with the beginning of Advent. We made a fresh cut wreath from a fir or a spruce and put four candles on top of it and placed it on our kitchen table. On the fourth Sunday before Christmas, we lit the first candle. Then each night until Christmas, my family gathered around the table and sang Christmas songs and listened to Christmas stories. . . . Advent was a time of anticipation and hope, and it brought a special feeling into our humble home as we

An Advent wreath can consist of a simple evergreen wreath, three purple candles, a pink or rose-colored candle, and perhaps a central white candle.

prepared for something holy and beautiful. Each Sunday we lit one additional candle; by the fourth Sunday our expectations for the coming joyous events had reached their peak."[2]

In 2002, our family decided to incorporate Advent into our own Christmas traditions, and it became a particular favorite of our daughter, Rachel. She was five at the time, and I remember how much I enjoyed explaining to her the symbolism of the small wreath that we had purchased, describing how the wreath represents the never-ending circle of God's love, showing that he is the same forever in his love toward his people. The green of the wreath represents, as it does in the Christmas tree, the hope of eternal life that comes through Christ and serves as a reminder of the freshness of God's love and promises. The light of the candles reminds us that Jesus is the Light of the World, that his birth represented the coming of that light into darkness, and that we are called to reflect that light in our lives.

Traditionally the four candles of an Advent wreath are purple, the color of royalty, although one is sometimes pink or rose-colored. We decided to include the central, white candle in our wreath, which we light on Christmas Eve and again on Christmas Day. Each Sunday before Christmas an additional candle is lit, creating a beautiful stepped effect as the previous weeks' candles burn down farther. After lighting each candle, we take turns reading scriptures that illustrate Advent themes, which we draw from the Book of Mormon as well as from the Old and New Testaments. After singing a carol, we have family prayer, and then proceed to less solemn traditions, like opening the day's pocket in our Advent calendar and enjoying a treat together.[3]

Traditions differ regarding the symbolism of the candles, but a common one is that they represent the hope, love, joy, and peace that come through Jesus Christ. Because these themes accord nicely with the major messages of Matthew 1–2 and Luke 1–2, I have included a reflection on these Advent themes after each chapter of this book. The addition of a central white candle has allowed us to weave a fifth theme into our Advent tradition, the salvation that comes through Christ, a reflection on which follows the final chapter about Christmas prophecies in the Book of Mormon.

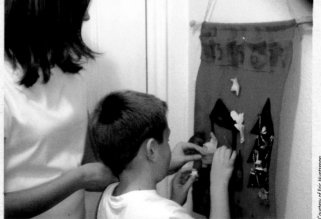

Rachel and Samuel enjoy the tradition of using an Advent calendar during the exciting countdown to Christmas.

1

SON OF DAVID

Matthew 1

Joseph, thou son of David, fear not to take unto thee Mary thy wife: for that which is conceived in her is of the Holy Ghost. And she shall bring forth a son, and thou shalt call his name JESUS: for he shall save his people from their sins.

—Matthew 1:20–21

The familiar Christmas story told in so many homes on Christmas Eve is actually a composite of two different biblical accounts, those of Matthew and of Luke, who alone of the biblical authors preserve detailed narratives about our Savior's birth. Matthew's and Luke's use of other scriptures in their Infancy Narratives encouraged early Christians to find other scriptural allusions to the Savior's promised coming. These, together with creative and often imaginative efforts in the first centuries after Christ, resulted in additional details being added to the traditional story that are not strictly part of the biblical Christmas accounts. Drawing on all these elements, the combined story has provided material for artistic and musical depictions of Jesus' birth through the centuries. But the Infancy Narratives themselves, together with prophecies from the Book of Mormon, remain the most powerful testimonies of our Savior's first advent.[1]

The narratives contained in Matthew 1–2 and Luke 1–2 present two very different accounts of the Savior's birth. While it is true that the two Nativity stories are largely complementary and agree on the most significant details, reading them separately helps us better understand the objectives and important insights of both authors while better appreciating the literary artistry of each. For instance, upon a careful reading of the two narratives, it becomes apparent that Matthew's account largely focuses on the role of Joseph, while much of Luke's story often reflects the perspective or character of Mary. Still, this observation alone does not explain all the differences in the

St. Joseph with Infant Jesus, *by Guido Reni. Hermitage, St. Petersburg, Russia/Courtesy of Art Resource, NY.*

> ## Episodes of Matthew 1
>
> - **The Story of Jesus' Genealogy** (Matthew 1:1–17)
>   - Abraham to David (Matthew 1:2–5)
>   - David to the Babylonian exile (Matthew 1:6–11)
>   - The exile to Joseph, "the husband of Mary" (Matthew 1:12–16)
> - **The Annunciation to Joseph** (Matthew 1:18–21)
>   - Prophecy fulfilled: "They shall call his name Emmanuel" (Matthew 1:22–23 fulfills Isaiah 7:14)
> - **The birth and naming of Jesus** (Matthew 1:24–25)

two accounts, leaving some discrepancies that are not easily harmonized. Nevertheless, both records "testify of the same basic truths: the coming of Jesus Christ into the world was long-prophesied, His mother was a pure and chosen vessel, His conception was divine, and His birth was miraculous" (see Appendix 1: The Infancy Narratives and the Christmas Story).[2]

Matthew and Luke accomplish this by using a series of different episodes or scenes—individual stories, if you will—that together illuminate specific aspects of Jesus' identity and mission. Attempts to harmonize the Infancy Narratives, both anciently and in recent times, often begin with the scenes first presented in Luke 1. This is because the stories of Jesus' forerunner, John the Baptist (Luke 1:5–25), and of Gabriel's annunciation to Mary (Luke 1:26–38), came before the angelic announcement to Joseph that his espoused wife was pregnant "by the power of the Holy Ghost" (Alma 7:10; see also Matthew 1:18–21).[3] However, there are reasons to begin our journey through the stories surrounding the Savior's birth with Matthew. His Gospel was probably written before Luke's, and it appears first in the canon. More important, Matthew's Infancy Narrative begins with a genealogy of Jesus, a pedigree which evokes promises made to Abraham and David centuries before the opening episodes recounted in Luke 1. By focusing on Jesus' role as the Son of David, the angel's annunciation to Joseph followed by the succinct description of Jesus' birth and naming remind us of these ancient promises.

THE STORY OF JESUS' GENEALOGY

Jesus' family background is a natural place for an author to begin his account of Jesus' birth, but Matthew's genealogy of Jesus (Matthew 1:1–17) is not one of the Christmas stories that tends to attract much attention at Christmastime. Rarely is it the subject of a sacrament meeting talk in The Church of Jesus Christ of Latter-day Saints, the topic of a Christmas sermon in other denominations, or the focus of holiday scripture study in our homes. This is no doubt partly because the succession of mostly unknown figures begetting generation after generation is, in many ways, reminiscent of the long genealogies in Genesis, Numbers, 1 Chronicles, Ezra, and even the book of Ether. When reading such genealogies, we understand that they are somehow important, but because this type of narrative is not as exciting and interesting as others—particularly when compared with the other stories in the Infancy Narratives—we are tempted to skip or skim over the genealogy given in Matthew 1 when studying the Christmas story.[4]

Old Testament genealogies, however, served an important function in establishing kinship, confirming a family's position in the House of Israel, and validating claims to important royal or priestly positions.[5] In that regard, the genealogy that Matthew uses as the beginning of his Infancy Narrative, and indeed as the beginning of his Gospel, provides an important bridge between the Old and the New Testament. Some questions about this genealogy still remain unanswered, such as where Matthew got his information and how accurate it was in some of its lesser-known details.

For instance, did he have access to official archives, family traditions, or popularly circulating genealogies, and were these complete and always correct?

The organization of what material he had, however, reveals that Matthew had clear objectives that influenced how he selected and structured the information contained in the genealogy he records. Thus, what is most important in Matthew's genealogy is not necessarily found in its comprehensiveness or its absolute accuracy. Rather, what is important is how that genealogy establishes *who* the baby Jesus was and *what* he would do. Furthermore, both the familiar *and* the less well-known characters in it teach us valuable lessons. Matthew's arrangement of this genealogical material reveals important stories in itself, stories about the promises made to Abraham, the covenant that the Lord made with David, and God's interaction with people throughout the history of the Old Testament. Each of these stories had significance for Matthew's original readers and for us, his modern audience.[6]

A Jesse Tree, *by Girolamo Genga. In this sixteenth-century painting attributed to Girolamo Genga, the descendants of Jesse, the father of King David, are depicted as a tree that grows out of Jesse's loins. At the top of the tree sit Mary and the Baby Jesus.*

Matthew's account of Jesus' genealogy begins with the words "The book of the generations of *Jesus Christ,* the son of *David,* the son of *Abraham*" (Matthew 1:1; emphasis added). These three names provide pivotal points of reference for the genealogy, which proceeds in descending order from Abraham to David (Matthew 1:2–5), then from David to the Babylonian exile (Matthew 1:6–11), and finally from the exile to Joseph, the husband of Mary (Matthew 1:12–16). Abraham's significance is seen first in his role as the father of God's covenant people. God's promises to Abraham are recounted in

Genesis 12–17, with a focus on specific covenants that God made with him in regard to the promised land and his numerous posterity (see Genesis 15:18–21; 17:1–16, 21). The importance that the Jews of Jesus' day placed on being the seed of Abraham is seen in their claims to Jesus later in his ministry (see Matthew 3:9; Luke 3:8; John 8:33). Matthew's genealogy thus begins by making it clear that Jesus was in Abraham's promised line.

However, one of the earliest promises that the Lord made with Abraham was that in his seed *"all* families of the earth [should]be blessed" (Genesis 12:3; emphasis added; see also Genesis 22:18). The expansion of this promise in Abraham 2:10–11 makes it clear that an important aspect of the Abrahamic covenant is that as many as accept the gospel, both Israelites and Gentiles, are counted as the seed of Abraham and become heirs of the blessings of the priesthood. Significantly, Paul, writing in the century after Jesus' birth, taught that this blessing came to all nations through Christ himself, who was the seed of Abraham in a very specific way (Galatians 3:14, 16). In other words, while much of Jesus' genealogy focuses on his role as the Son of David and the king of Israel, the reference to Abraham can also be seen as expanding his role as a blessing to all nations and peoples.[7] This is an important aspect of the rest of Matthew's Gospel, because although overall his Gospel comes from the perspective of a Jewish author writing for a Jewish audience, he also seems to have been writing when a growing number of Gentiles were coming into the Church, and there are important references to Gentiles in his Gospel.[8] Thus the emphasis on Abraham stresses the importance of Jesus to both Jew *and* Gentile.

Matthew begins the second section of the genealogy by noting, "And Jesse begat *David the king;* and David the king begat Solomon . . ." (Matthew 1:6; emphasis added). This section features not only David and Solomon but, with a few exceptions, all of the other succeeding kings of Judah; however, only David is referred to as "the king." This reinforces the idea that David was the greatest and most successful king of ancient Israel, and as such provided the standard for his successors to follow. Though his failings and mistakes are well-known, David was recognized for always being faithful to YHWH, or Jehovah. As a result, the Lord made a covenant with David, promising that he would establish his kingdom through David's direct posterity and "[establish] the throne of his kingdom for ever" (2 Samuel 7:13). While this Old Testament passage continues by applying that covenant in the first instance to David's immediate successor, Solomon, it ends by stressing again that the Lord will keep this covenant in perpetuity, telling David that "thine house and thy kingdom shall be established for ever before thee: thy throne shall be established for ever" (2 Samuel 7:16).

Matthew's reference to the exile in Babylon emphasizes that the kingdom of Judah came to an end when David's descendants lost the throne (Matthew 1:11–12), but Matthew prepares us to see that the Lord's covenant with David would be realized in another way. This is revealed in the third section of the genealogy, which concludes with Jesus, "who is called *Christ*" (Matthew 1:16; emphasis added). By using this title, Matthew indicates that despite the loss of the worldly kingdom, Jesus is not only David's rightful heir but is in fact the messianic culmination of the promises made to David. The term

Corelli's *Concerto Grosso in G Minor*
"The Christmas Concerto"

While singing and listening to familiar carols is a common pastime in the Christmas season, listening to some of the longer musical masterworks can also be a wonderful way to bring the Spirit into our holiday preparations and celebration. One of my favorites is the *Concerto Grosso in G Minor* by Arcangelo Corelli (1653–1713). It is an instrumental rather than a vocal work, which allows the listener to be moved merely by the music rather than by any words, invoking the Christmas spirit in a different way. An important composition of the early Baroque period, it had a direct influence on later and, to our time, better-known composers such as Bach and Handel.

Corelli inscribed *"fatto per la note di Natale,"* or, "made for a Christmas night," at the top of the score, earning the composition the nickname "The Christmas Concerto." The idea of a Christmas concerto arose from an Italian folk custom in which rustic farmers and shepherds would act out the Nativity scene in neighboring towns. Their reenactment was often accompanied by music on traditional instruments. Drawing upon this tradition, Corelli created a masterpiece in which two violins and a viola play against a small orchestral ensemble. The *Concerto Grosso in G Minor* consists of seven movements, with the final section, the Largo, serving as a pastoral movement that represents the shepherds' adoration of the Christ Child. Such pastoral movements, of which perhaps Handel's later *Pastoral Symphony* is most famous, were played regularly in churches on Christmas Eve.[9]

The Orchestra at Temple Square performs with the Mormon Tabernacle Choir during its annual Christmas concert.

The mosaics of the south dome of the narthex, or outer hall, of the Byzantine Chora Church in Istanbul, depict the genealogy of Jesus. The Savior appears in the center as Christ Pantocrator, or "ruler of all," while his royal ancestors surround him at the base of the dome.

Christ literally means "the anointed one" (Hebrew, *māšîaḥ,* Greek, *Christos*). While the Davidic kings and properly installed high priests were all originally anointed and hence had all been "messiahs," by the time of Jesus, the promised Son of David who would be the ultimate future king came to be seen as *the* Messiah.[10] Thus, in Jesus was born the messianic king who would rule and reign in Israel forever, thereby truly fulfilling God's covenant with David.

This emphasis on Jesus as the Davidic Messiah helps explain the importance of the expression "Son of David" in Matthew. While it occurs four times each in Mark and Luke, its use is a particular feature of Matthew's Gospel, where it appears ten times. Its importance is emphasized in Matthew's Infancy Narrative, both in the genealogy and in the following section.[11] Matthew emphasizes the overarching importance of Jesus' Davidic heritage by suggesting the name "David" in the very structure of his genealogy. Summarizing the pedigree, Matthew writes, "So all the generations from Abraham to David are *fourteen* generations; and from David until the carrying away into Babylon are *fourteen* generations;

and from the carrying away into Babylon unto Christ are *fourteen* generations" (Matthew 1:17; emphasis added). David's name, in the Hebrew system of *gematria,* adds up to fourteen.[12] While Greek is the language of the text of Matthew's Gospel and we have no indication that he wrote an earlier version in either Hebrew or Aramaic, this Hebrew construction would still have been well-known to Matthew and presumably most of his audience.

The structure of three sections of fourteen seems more important than some of the list's details. The three periods of time covered by the genealogy represent unequal amounts of time—roughly 750, 400, and 600 years respectively. Not only are these allegedly equal divisions not likely historically, they do not all also consist strictly of fourteen generations. The first has thirteen generations with fourteen different men listed; the second has fourteen generations with fourteen men; and the third has thirteen generations with fourteen men, and only because the first listed, Jeconias (the Old Testament Jehoiachin, also known as Jeconiah), is repeated from the end of the second section. Further, Matthew has also omitted names in the first and second sections that are otherwise known from the Old Testament. Matthew apparently needed to be selective to achieve the repeating structure of fourteen generations to produce the Davidic symbolism in the repeated number fourteen.[13] Nevertheless, Matthew's selectivity does not change the fundamental truths that he sought

Courtesy of Bridgeman Art Library. Used by permission.

Betrothal of the Holy Virgin and St. Joseph, *by James Tissot.*

Luke's Different Genealogy

The Gospel of Luke provides a genealogy for Jesus that is substantially different than that which Matthew records. Whereas Matthew uses his genealogy to begin his Infancy Narrative, Luke delays listing Jesus' ancestors until Luke 3:23–38, placing his genealogy between Jesus' baptism and the account of his being tempted in the wilderness. Luke's genealogy is structurally different, ascending from Jesus "being (as was supposed) the son of Joseph" (Luke 3:23) up to Adam, "which was the son of God" (Luke 3:30), rather than descending from Abraham through David to Joseph as Matthew's does. Going back to Adam reflects Luke's wider outlook. His Gospel focuses more on the inclusion of the Gentiles in Christ's mission than does Matthew's. Furthermore, where Matthew's genealogy stresses that Jesus was the Son of David, the closing statement in Luke's account emphasizes Jesus' identity as the Son of God, a point emphasized earlier in Luke's account of Jesus' baptism, when God pronounced, "Thou art my beloved Son" (Luke 3:22).

However, the most obvious and difficult-to-explain discrepancy between the genealogies is in the substantially different names that occur in the two lists. Matthew traces Davidic descent through the recognized royal line from David to Solomon and then through the kings of Judah. Luke, on the other hand, charts the descent through David's son Nathan, perhaps reflecting the prophecy that no descendant of Jehoiakim, one of the last successors of David through Solomon, would sit on the throne of David (see Jeremiah 36:30). The lists briefly converge again with the figures of Salathiel (Shealtiel) and Zorobabel (Zerubbabel), descendants of David who returned from the Babylonian exile, but then they diverge again, continuing with different names all the way to Joseph's father, whom Luke names Heli (Eli) rather than Jacob.

Various attempts have been made to reconcile some or all of the differences between the two lists. As early as the Christian church father Julius Africanus (circa A.D. 160–240), the difference in the name of Joseph's father was explained through the practice of Levirate marriage, whereby the widow of a man who had died childless was married to the deceased husband's brother, with any offspring from the second marriage attributed to the first husband. By this argument, the Jacob mentioned by Matthew died childless and his wife then married Jacob's half-brother (who therefore had a different father) Heli, who actually fathered Joseph. Taking another approach, Annius of Viterbo proposed in 1490 that Heli was Joseph's father-in-law rather than his father. While this option ignores the construction of Luke 3:23, which clarifies that Joseph was the son and not the son-in-law of Heli, the possibility that Luke's genealogy follows that of Mary remains attractive to many because this would demonstrate that Jesus was the literal as well as legal descendant of David.[14] Another explanation posits that Matthew's account represents Joseph's (and hence Jesus') legal genealogy in terms of royal succession, while Luke's account attempts to record his actual or biological lineage. This too, is an attractive explanation, but it would require that the line from Solomon to Jehoiakim died out, at which point the line somehow passed to Nathan through Shealtiel and Zerubbabel, and then this branch also lapsed.[15]

Many scholars propose that Matthew and Luke simply used different, competing genealogical lists of descendants of David that were circulating at the time in order to emphasize different concepts, in particular, (1) that Jesus was the Son of David and heir to the promises of Abraham (Matthew) and, (2) that he was the Son of God and belonged to the entire human family (Luke).[16] While the details of the lists are different and remain difficult to reconcile, the points where they do agree represent the most important theological truths: namely that Jesus, through both Joseph and perhaps Mary, was heir to the covenants and promises that God made with Abraham and David.

to establish: The miraculous baby of this Infancy Narrative was the son of Abraham, a blessing both to Israel and to all nations, and above all the Son of David.

At the same time, the story of Jesus' genealogy recalls other Old Testament stories, each of which displays God's providence in raising up Jesus and shows the roles that individuals played in that plan. For instance, names in the first section, such as the patriarchs Isaac and Jacob, immediately call to mind the Lord's renewal of his covenant with Abraham's heirs. In both of these cases, the sons receiving the promises were not the firstborn, Ishmael having been born before Isaac and Esau before Jacob. Likewise Judah, through whose tribe kings and eventually the Messiah sprang, was the fourth son of Jacob, not the first. Rather than being the result of natural birthright, the favored status of these figures was the result of their own faithfulness and, to a certain extent, the individual unrighteousness of their older siblings. The favoring of younger children also reflects the exercise of God's sovereign will, demonstrating his right to choose whom he would.

With only a few exceptions, such as Ezekias and Josias (Old Testament "Hezekiah" and "Josiah"), the kings of the second section of Matthew's genealogy made damaging mistakes or displayed outright wickedness, showing that the Lord can nonetheless bring good out of bad and that he always keeps his promises, even when his mortal covenant partners fail to keep theirs. In contrast to these royal and often infamous figures, most of the characters in the third section, from the return from the Babylonian captivity to Joseph, are completely unknown. Their presence in the genealogy of Jesus illustrates how God can work through the most common and unremarkable of people, and not just through the kingly and prominent.[17]

Perhaps the most intriguing stories suggested by the Matthean genealogy of Jesus, however, are those evoked by the inclusion of four women in the list of Jesus' ancestors. The very presence of these women in the catalog is unexpected, because lineage was generally traced through the man's line alone, with women rarely appearing in Old Testament genealogies. Even more surprising are the particular women whom Matthew mentions: Thamar (Matthew 1:3; "Tamar" in Genesis 38:6–30), Rachab (Matthew 1:5; "Rahab" in Joshua 2:1–22), Ruth (Matthew 1:5; Ruth 2–4), and the wife of Uriah the Hittite (Matthew 1:6; "Bathsheba" in 2 Samuel 11–12). On the one hand, their personal lives were

"He Is the Root and the Offspring of David"

Though it is not a Christmas carol, the final movement of Robert Cundick's LDS oratorio *The Redeemer* (see Chapter 5: Further Glad Tidings) provides an apt musical commentary on both Matthew's genealogy of Jesus and the reason for which Jesus came into the world even as it points our minds forward to his return. In the conclusion to a sacred service of music about Jesus Christ's mission, the chorus sings a text taken from Revelation 22:16–17 and 22:20:

[He is] the root and the offspring of David,
And the bright and morning star.

And the Spirit and the bride, say Come.
And let him who heareth say, Come.

And let him that is athirst come.
Let him take the water of life freely.
He which testifieth these things saith,
Surely, I come quickly. . . .
Even so, come, Lord Jesus.[18]

The opening lines, stressing Jesus' Davidic heritage, also employ star imagery, and singing or hearing them in a Christmas context anticipates the star of Bethlehem in Matthew 2. The central stanza alludes to the Church, in its role as the Bride of Christ, welcoming the Savior and bidding all who wish to partake of his salvation to come unto him. But it is the final verse, which looks forward to Jesus' glorious return, that gives our annual Christmas celebration an additional level of meaning. As we commemorate his birth each year in our holiday celebrations, we should remember that our joy in his first coming should prefigure the even greater joy we will feel at his Second Coming.

suspect, or in the case of Ruth, might have been seen as being suspect (Ruth 3:6–9), which has led some to suggest that their inclusion shows that sinners, too, had a part in how and why Jesus came into the world. On the other hand, these women also seem to have come from outside the House of Israel: The first two were probably Canaanites, the third a Moabite, and the fourth perhaps a Hittite, like her husband. This ethnic consideration thus indicates that Gentiles also have a part in Jesus. But most important, all four of these women share something important with Mary, the fifth woman in the list of Jesus' forebears (Matthew 1:12–16). All of them played an important role—and often an unusual role—in bringing the Savior into the world, showing the significance of women in God's plan and fulfilling the promise that it would be through Eve's seed—that it is, through the offspring of a woman, Mary, but not a mortal man—that the devil would at last be overcome (see Genesis 3:15).[19]

JOSEPH'S STORY

Despite the importance of women—especially Mary—in the genealogy given by Matthew, the last figure in the *direct* line from Abraham and David down to the time of Jesus was neither Mary nor

Jesus but rather Joseph, who despite his royal ancestry was known as a simple carpenter (see Matthew 13:55). The Greek word translated as carpenter is *tektōn,* which can mean any type of craftsman or artisan, perhaps even a stoneworker in a place such as the Holy Land where stone was more common as a building material than wood. In Greek literature, however, it is most commonly used for a worker in wood, and Joseph the Carpenter has become a familiar figure in art and tradition.[20] In the context of first-century Judea and Galilee, such a craftsman could have been either a skilled artisan working in his own shop or an itinerant worker, taking whatever day labor he could engage.

Joseph's home and carpentry shop came to be commemorated at the site now occupied by the Church of St. Joseph in Nazareth.[21] This small town, of perhaps no more than 400 people, was only a few miles from the large, hellenized town of Sepphoris, where much construction occurred in the first century. While Joseph—and later Jesus, who also is described as a *tektōn* (Mark 6:3)—might have found regular work in this neighboring town, Joseph's occupation is not emphasized or even mentioned in the Infancy Narrative.[22] Nor does Matthew give any other details, such as where Joseph was living when his story opened. In fact, if Matthew 2 is read without Luke's account in mind, one might conclude that Joseph and his family were from Bethlehem, the city of David.

Jesus is connected to Joseph in the genealogy because ancient practice always traced legal descent through the male line. As a result, even though Joseph was not the actual father of Jesus, he needed to be the adoptive father of the promised child for Jesus to be a recognized as a "son of David." However, to accomplish this, Matthew must break his pattern at the end of the genealogy, connecting Joseph to Jesus not through an act of begetting but rather by his relationship to Jesus' mother alone, noting that Joseph was "the husband of Mary, of whom was born Jesus, who is called the Christ" (Matthew 1:16).

Courtesy of Chad Emmett.

An Arab groom rides a donkey to his wedding in modern-day Nazareth.

Mary is often held to have been of the house of David somehow as well, in which case the marriage of Mary and Joseph might have been between cousins or other relatives, making Jesus a literal descendant of David also (see Acts 2:30, 13:23; Romans 1:3, 15:12; Galatians 4:4; Revelation 22:16).[23] Nevertheless, the emphasis in Matthew's account of Joseph's story is on how he, as a descendant of David, was chosen to accept Mary's son as his own, legally claiming him and thus being willing to raise and protect the Son of God.

Courtesy of Kerry Muhlestein.

A modern actor depicts a biblical carpenter in the Nazareth Historical Village in a shop with tools reminiscent of those used by Joseph.

The first scene in Joseph's story begins with a description of the circumstances of Jesus' birth: "Now the birth of Jesus Christ was on this wise . . ." This entire episode (Matthew 1:18–21) can be termed "the Annunciation to Joseph," because like the better-known Annunciation to Mary (Luke 1:26–38), an angel appears announcing the coming miraculous birth of Jesus. Yet while the angel in Luke's account reveals to Mary that she will be the mother of the Son of God, Matthew notes that Joseph first discovers Mary's pregnancy through more conventional means and after the fact: "When as his mother Mary was *espoused* to Joseph, before they came together, she was *found* with child of the Holy Ghost" (Matthew 1:18; emphasis added). The term Matthew uses for *espoused* (Greek, *mnēsteutheisēs*) means "betrothed" or "engaged," but in context of first-century Judaism it referred to a binding, legal contract that carried all the restrictions of marriage while still anticipating the couple's marriage ceremony, after which they would live together. Thus when Mary was found to be pregnant before she and Joseph had begun their married life together, this was tantamount to her being guilty of adultery.[24]

Matthew's explanation that Mary was pregnant "of the Holy Ghost" (Greek, *ek pneumatos hagiou*) is an aside to Matthew's readers, because Joseph does not understand the divine nature of the baby's conception until the angel subsequently explains it to him. The phrase in Greek is somewhat unusual,

Anxiety of St. Joseph, by James Tissot.

and its rendering in the English of the King James Bible can be misleading. First, in this context, the use of the preposition *ek,* meaning literally "out of," suggests source, origin, or motivation rather than agency. Further, the phrase lacks the definite article "the" (Greek, *tou*), so rather than referring to *the* Holy Ghost, the sense may be that the source of Mary's pregnancy was the more general holy power or the spirit of God (see Alma 7:10).[25] That Jesus was the Son of God and not somehow the offspring or creation of the Holy Ghost is clear both from his being called "the Son of God" elsewhere in the Gospels and from latter-day sources.[26]

Matthew describes Joseph as a "just man" (Greek, *dikaios,* meaning "upright" or one who keeps the law fully). Understanding his rights as a seemingly wronged fiancé but not wanting to see Mary publicly punished or humiliated, he seeks to annul their contract privately.[27] At this point an angel intercedes, in Matthew's account appearing to Joseph in a dream. The Joseph Smith Translation suggests that this was, in fact a "vision" (JST, Matthew 2:3). However, because visions sometimes come in the form of dreams (see 1 Nephi 8:2), perhaps the Prophet's clarification was meant to emphasize that Joseph in fact had a revelatory and not just an ordinary dream. Joseph's receiving revelation in dreams—both here and later in Matthew 2:13 and 2:19—creates a literary echo with another Joseph who was famous for having and interpreting revelatory dreams: the Old Testament figure of Joseph in Egypt (Genesis 37:5–11; 40:5–23; 41:1–36). The name *Yosef* that the two share means "YHWH (Jehovah) will add." The parallels between the two men are underscored in Matthew's genealogy, in which Joseph the Carpenter is the son of a Jacob (Matthew 1:16), just as the first Joseph was the son of the patriarch Jacob.

Yet, more significant than this parallelism is the fact that the angel who visits Joseph the Carpenter in his dream identifies Joseph according to his Davidic heritage. Directing him not to put Mary away, the angel says, "Joseph, *thou son of David,* fear not to take unto thee Mary thy wife" (Matthew 1:20; emphasis added). The angel's applying this title to Joseph connects this scene with the preceding genealogy, showing why its symbolic emphasis on the name *David* is realized through Joseph and suggests that Matthew's genealogy focuses primarily on Jesus' legal or royal descent.

Mary's child, however, is to be more than another descendant of David, of which there may have been many by the first century. Rather, the child's future role as Savior is clear from the angel's next directive to Joseph, "thou shalt call his name JESUS: for he shall save his people from their sins" (Matthew 1:21). The English name Jesus comes from *Iēsous,* which is the Greek form of the Hebrew name *Yəhôšûa* (Yehoshua), which in later biblical Hebrew was often contracted to *Yēšûaʿ* (Yeshua). Both of these forms, usually rendered in the King James Version of the Old Testament as Joshua,

Annunciation to Joseph, *by Joseph Brickey.*

have the meaning of "YHWH (or Jehovah) saves." However, while the most famous Old Testament Joshua frequently delivered his people in battle, this new Joshua would in fact be Jehovah himself, ultimately defeating Satan and delivering his people from both sin and death.

Matthew sees Joseph's naming the child Jesus as being the fulfillment of Isaiah 7:14, thereby further underscoring the divine nature of the promised baby and alluding to the miraculous nature of his conception: "Now all this was done, that it might be fulfilled which was spoken of the Lord by his prophet, saying, Behold, a *virgin* shall be with child, . . . and they shall call his name Emmanuel, which being interpreted is, *God with us*" (Matthew 1:22–23; emphasis added). This is the first example in Matthew's Gospel of a "formula quotation" (see "Formula Quotations in Matthew" in this chapter), and it is also a case in which Matthew uses an Old Testament reference to make a

While a church commemorating the annunciation to Joseph has existed on this site in Nazareth since the Byzantine period, the Franciscans built the current Church of St. Joseph in 1914.

theological point. While *'almâ,* the Hebrew word used in Isaiah 7:14 for "virgin," can mean a literal virgin, it commonly means simply a young girl. Further, in the original context of Isaiah's prophecy, some have applied the prediction to a child in Isaiah's own day, probably King Ahaz's son Hezekiah. The son of a new, young wife, Hezekiah promised to be one of the rare righteous kings of Judah, and in many ways he was an anticipation of Christ.

Joseph and Jesus, Our Children and Us

© Simon Dewey. Used by permission.

In the Arms of Joseph, by Simon Dewey.

The story of how Joseph the Carpenter accepted, protected, raised, and no doubt loved a precious child who was not his own is one that stirs the heart. In many traditions, his goodness and the faithful discharge of his special mission earned him the title Saint Joseph, and he is honored together with Mary and the Baby Jesus as part of a Holy Family. After the Infancy Narratives of Matthew and Luke and the brief story of the boy Jesus in the temple, Joseph is never heard of again. Passing references to Jesus' supposed father (Matthew 13:55; Mark 6:3; John 6:42), together with his otherwise conspicuous absence later in the Gospels seem to suggest that he was no longer alive when the adult Jesus began his public ministry. We are left instead with the impression of a very good man, the loving husband of a special woman and the guardian of a precious child.

Those who have adopted or fostered the children of others may identify particularly with Joseph. But those of us who have biological children of our own or even those who have not yet been blessed with any children can still learn a dear lesson from the example of Joseph. In a real sense, none of our children are our own. Priceless spirit children of Heavenly Parents, all children on this earth are only here on loan from a loving God who trusts us all—parents, grandparents, family, friends, even strangers—to protect, care for, teach, and love them.

Occasionally on Christmas Eve I give each member of my family a card depicting Mary with Jesus, or Joseph with Jesus. We each take some time to write on the back of the card some gift that we will give the Savior in the coming year. Without fail, looking at an artistic depiction of Joseph fills me with a great sense of duty and gratitude. Looking at the image of Mary underscores for me that Elaine is not just my wife; she is herself a daughter of God. Thinking of how I hope some man will one day treat my own daughter, Rachel, I realize how my Father in Heaven wants me to treat Elaine. In other words, God is not just my Heavenly Father; he is, in a sense, also my father-in-law. As I look at my own precious children, I feel, like Joseph, that I have been entrusted with a great treasure. Recognizing that Joseph was a strong, responsible, and loving man who sought and received revelation to care for his family, I am inspired to emulate those qualities. In those moments, the gift I hope to give my Lord that year is to be more like Joseph the Carpenter.

Formula Quotations in Matthew

An important feature of the Gospel of Matthew is its frequent use of Old Testament scripture. While all the Gospels make references to Old Testament passages, in at least fourteen instances Matthew does it in a very specific way, introducing a direct quotation by stating that something in the life of Jesus specifically fulfilled Old Testament prophecy. Because Matthew is often seen as a Jewish writer writing for Jews, it is tempting to consider these "formula quotations" as attempts to prove to a Jewish audience that Jesus' life was the fulfillment of Jewish prophecy. However, it is just as likely that the quotations were intended to strengthen early Christians in their own faith.

The passages that follow the opening formulas are often direct quotations from the Septuagint, the Greek translation of the Hebrew Bible. In other instances, Matthew seems to have done his own translation from a Hebrew original, which at times seems to be similar to the later traditional Hebrew text used by the translators of the King James Version of the Old Testament but on occasion represents earlier, otherwise unknown variants. The slight variations that arise in Matthew's quotations attest the fluidity that existed in Old Testament scripture before it was standardized in later centuries. Perhaps more significantly, the readings Matthew adopted reveal his intention to use the formula quotations to teach meaningful truths about Jesus, as is seen in his decision to follow the Septuagint's rendition of "virgin" in Isaiah 7:14.

Five of Matthew's fourteen formula quotations appear in his Infancy Narrative. In addition to the citation of Isaiah 7:14 in Matthew 1:22–23, they are:

- 2 Samuel 5:2 and Micah 5:2 in Matthew 2:5–6;
- Hosea 11:1 in Matthew 2:15;
- Jeremiah 31:15 in Matthew 2:17–18;
- and an uncertain citation in Matthew 2:23 (perhaps a reference to Judges 16:17, Isaiah 4:3, or Isaiah 11:1; see Chapter 4: King of Israel).[28]

Matthew, however, chose to translate the Hebrew term from Isaiah with the Greek word *parthenos*, which specifically means "virgin." He is not alone in this choice, since the Septuagint, or Greek translation of the Old Testament, had made the same word choice some two centuries before, suggesting that the idea of a virgin miraculously conceiving was, in fact, an early interpretation.[29] Matthew thus sees the ultimate fulfillment of Isaiah's prophecy in Jesus and by his application of this passage teaches the vital truth that Jesus was not actually Joseph's son but was, in fact, divinely conceived. He then supplies an interpretation of the Hebrew term *'Immānû'ēl*, explaining that it means "God with us." In other words, the child would not just be the Son of God; he would be, in a very real sense, divine himself and was coming to be ever with his people. Matthew stresses that Jesus taught this after his

"Joseph Dearest, Joseph Mine"

One of the most popular Christmas songs in Germany, this tune has been sung to two different texts, *Resonet in laudibus*, the earliest copy of which dates to between 1355 and 1360, and *Joseph, Lieber Joseph Mein*, which may be as old as 1400. Frequently sung after the Reformation in Lutheran communion services on Christmas Eve, it was also sung at weddings because the loving relationship between Joseph and Mary seemed to typify the ideal Christian marriage. In harmony with Matthew's focus on the figure of Joseph the Carpenter, the role that the lyrics paint for Joseph is a fitting tribute to the man chosen to be the protector of the Son of God.[30]

Various translations of the text and several settings of the tune circulate in English-speaking circles, but perhaps the one best-known to Latter-day Saint audiences is the text adapted by Mack Wilberg in his arrangement of this beautiful carol:

Joseph dearest, Joseph mine,
Help to rock this Child divine;
God hath sent in His own time,
A Son, a babe,
The Holy One of Mary!

. . . .

He came to us in Bethlehem,
He came to us a spotless gem,
He came to us our Lord to be,
Little, humble Babe indeed,
Lowly Child be Thou our need.

Sleep, Thou dear and lovely one,
Come to earth as God's own Son,
For this day all love is won
With Thee, the Son,
The Holy One of Mary!

For Christ, our Lord, is born this day,
Is born this day Immanuel.
Precious Child born in a lowly manger.
Eia, Eia, Glory be on high,
Sing Alleluia.[31]

Resurrection when he promised his disciples, "I am with you alway, even unto the end of the world" (Matthew 28:20).[32]

Still, to be the recognized "Son of David," Jesus needed to be Joseph's legal son. Ephrem the Syrian, some two centuries later, explained this in one of his Nativity hymns:

Why then was it necessary that she, a daughter of David,
be betrothed to Joseph and that then Your birth
from her would be without man?
The succession of kings is written in the name of men instead of women.
Joseph, a son of David, betrothed to a daughter of David,
for the child could not be registered in the name of His mother.[33]

Rising from his dream, Joseph followed the angel's instructions, accepting Mary as his lawful wife but abstaining from relations with her until after she "brought forth her firstborn son" (Matthew 1:24–25). While the tradition of Mary's supposed perpetual virginity began as early as the apocryphal text known as the *Protoevangelium of James* in the mid–second century, the final verse of Matthew simply maintains that Mary remained a virgin until after Jesus' birth in order to make it clear that Joseph was not the child's biological father.

Nevertheless, Joseph's naming of the child is generally seen as a legal act of recognition, accepting Jesus as his own son and agreeing to raise and protect him.[34] With this act of naming, Matthew draws together both the genealogy and Joseph's story, teaching in the process *who* the baby of the Christmas story was and *what* he would come to do. He was to be the seed of Abraham that would bless all people. He was to be the Son of David, who would ascend the throne of his father David and reign over the house of Israel. He was the Son of God, divinely and miraculously conceived by God's holy power to be "God with us." And ultimately he is Jehovah, who saves his people.

Reading the account of Jesus' genealogy together with Joseph's story helps prepare us for Christmas by reminding us not only who the promised baby would be but also that he came to be our King and our Savior. Beyond that, those in Jesus' pedigree remind us that all people—Jews and Gentiles, men and women, saints and sinners, the famous and the lesser-known—have a part in Jesus. So we too should do our part in helping to bring Jesus into the world in our day through our testimonies, our lives, and our examples. Likewise, the noble example of Joseph—of kingly lineage, though but a common carpenter or craftsman—reminds us that we are also of royal stock. As children of our God, we are called upon to fulfill our callings in this life, whatever our station, striving to be righteous and responsive to divine guidance. In particular we should be loving and protective of our spouses, children, and friends. ❖

THE ADVENT THEME OF HOPE

While the four Advent themes of hope, love, joy, and peace are sometimes celebrated in a different order than represented here, hope is almost always the theme celebrated on the first Sunday of Advent. As the first candle of an Advent wreath is lit, a family choosing to use this custom as a way of preparing for Christmas can thus use the occasion to remember how the Christmas story recalls the birth of the Promised King, an event prophesied and hoped for from the time of Adam until that first Christmas. An example of this hope is reflected in Matthew's genealogy of Jesus as well as in the angel's message to Joseph, promising the birth of Immanuel, or "God with us." But the celebration of Advent does not just remember Jesus' first coming. It can also celebrate his presence and importance in our lives *now* while also helping us look forward to his Second Coming.

Courtesy of Eric Huntsman

The first purple candle, celebrating the hope that comes through Jesus, is lit on the first Sunday of Advent.

Reading scriptures that reflect these aspects of the hope that we have in Jesus is a valuable part of a family celebration of Advent. Passages that our family regularly reads include the following:

"The Spirit of the Lord God is upon me; because *the Lord hath anointed me to preach good tidings* unto the meek; he hath sent me to bind up the brokenhearted, to proclaim liberty to the captives, and the opening of the prison to them that are bound; *to proclaim the acceptable year of the Lord*, and the day of vengeance of our God; to comfort all that mourn" (Isaiah 61:1–2; emphasis added).

"For, for this intent have we written these things, that they may know that we knew of Christ, and *we had a hope of his glory many hundred years before his coming*; and not only we ourselves had a hope of his glory, but also all the holy prophets which were before us. Behold, they believed in Christ and worshiped the Father in his name, and also we worship the Father in his name" (Jacob 4:4–5; emphasis added).

"Therefore being justified by faith, we have peace with God through our Lord Jesus Christ: by whom also we have access by faith into this grace wherein we stand, *and rejoice in hope of the glory of God*. And not only so, but we glory in tribulations also: *knowing that tribulation worketh patience; and patience, experience; and experience, hope*: and hope maketh not ashamed; because the love of God is shed abroad in our hearts by the Holy Ghost which is given unto us" (Romans 5:1–5; emphasis added).

"And what is it that ye shall hope for? Behold I say unto you that *ye shall have hope through the atonement of Christ and the power of his resurrection*, to be raised unto life eternal" (Moroni 7:41; emphasis added).

"For the Lord himself shall descend from heaven with a shout, with the voice of the archangel, and with the trump of God: and the dead in Christ shall rise first: *then we which are alive and remain shall be caught up together with them in the clouds, to meet the Lord in the air: and so shall we ever be with the Lord"* (1 Thessalonians 4:16–17; emphasis added).

The four Advent candles can also be used to represent the covenants that God has made with his people, reminding us of the importance of the covenants that we ourselves make with the Lord and assuring us that he will keep them. Accordingly, we use the lighting of the first candle as an opportunity to discuss with our children the covenants that God made with the patriarchs Adam, Enoch, and Noah. In particular, God saved Noah and his family from the flood and promised them life, just as we are saved through Christ and hope for eternal life through him.

The first Sunday of Advent is the time when our family sets up our Nativity scene. After our Advent wreath, the crèche is the first of the Christmas decorations to be set out, helping Rachel and Samuel focus on the true meaning of Christmas throughout the month.

Music is an important part of the celebration of Advent as it is of the Christmas season generally. In some traditions only carols especially meant for Advent are sung in the weeks leading up to Christmas, with Christmas carols themselves being reserved for Christmas Eve and the "Twelve Days of Christmas" that begin with Christmas Day. However, families can use any familiar carols for their home celebrations, though our family always opens our Christmas season by singing "O Come, O Come Emmanuel," which is the traditional carol for the beginning of Advent. The original Latin text dates back as early as the reign of Charlemagne (771–814). The English text and the now-familiar tune were not published until 1854, though the melody seems to have been based on an earlier French original.[1] Although there were originally seven verses, the following four are perhaps the most well-known:

O come, O come, Emmanuel,
And ransom captive Israel,
That mourns in lonely exile here
Until the Son of God appears.

Rejoice! Rejoice! Emmanuel
Shall come to thee O Israel.

O come, thou rod of Jesse, free
Thine own from Satan's tyranny.
From depths of hell thy people save
And give them vict'ry o'er the grave.

Chorus

O come, O Dayspring, come and cheer
Our spirits by thine advent here,
And drive away the shades of night
And pierce the clouds and bring us light.

. . . .

Chorus

O come, O come, Thou Lord of might
Who to thy tribes, on Sinai's height
In ancient times did'st give the law
In cloud and majesty and awe.

Chorus[2]

2
PROMISED SAVIOR

Luke 1

*And Mary said, My soul doth magnify the Lord, and my spirit
hath rejoiced in God my Saviour. For he hath regarded the low estate of his handmaiden:
for, behold, from henceforth all generations shall call me blessed.*

—Luke 1:46–48

While Matthew began his Infancy Narrative with a genealogy and then followed with succinct stories about the annunciation to Joseph and the birth of Jesus, Luke's narrative includes several dramatic scenes as a prelude to his later description of the Nativity. Overall, Luke's account gives more background than does Matthew's and includes "careful comparisons and contrasts, poetic expressions, and [more] fully developed characters"[1] (see Appendix 1: The Infancy Narratives and the Christmas Story). These characters include both men and women who—as did the men and women in Matthew's genealogy—connect Luke's Gospel to the Old Testament. Within the Infancy Narrative itself, the stories of these men and women give the account an intimate feel even as they heighten its drama. But above all, these characters are righteous Israelites who have prepared themselves for the parts that they will play by looking forward to Israel's promised Savior.

Luke begins his Infancy Narrative not with the story of Jesus' promised birth but rather with that of his forerunner, John the Baptist. He then uses this story as a literary foil—employing it to provide both comparisons and contrasts that place the story of Jesus in high relief. John's conception is also extraordinary, but Jesus' is divine and even more miraculous. And while John's birth brings joy and gladness to his family and their friends, it is but an overture to the more glorious and joyous birth of Jesus, recounted in Luke 2, that brings good tidings to all men and women.

ZACHARIAS'S STORY

Just as Zacharias's son, John the Baptist, would be a forerunner for Jesus,

---

*Meeting of Mary and Elisabeth, by
Carl Bloch. Courtesy Hope Gallery.*

Episodes of Luke 1

- The Annunciation to Zacharias (Luke 1:5–25)
- The Annunciation to Mary (Luke 1:26–38)
- The Visitation (Luke 1:39–56)
  ◦ Canticle: The *Magnificat* (Luke 1:46–55)
- The Birth of John the Baptist (Luke 1:57–80)
  ◦ Canticle: The *Benedictus* (Luke 1:68–79)

in a literary sense the visit of the angel Gabriel to the aged priest anticipates the annunciation to Mary. The name *Zacharias* in English is a transliteration of the Greek form of the Hebrew name *Zǝharyā* or "Zechariah," which means "YHWH (Jehovah) has remembered." John's father thus shared a name with a number of Old Testament figures, notably the prophet Zechariah, who was the son or grandson of Iddo, who prophesied about aspects of the Messiah's mission, especially regarding his glorious Second Coming (see Zechariah 13–14). Also sharing his name is the high priest Zechariah, the son of Jehoiada, who was martyred by wicked King Jehoash (2 Chronicles 24:20–22). This Zechariah was probably the one referred to by Jesus when he spoke of the "blood of Zacharias son of Barachias," who was slain "between the temple and the altar" (Matthew 23:35; see also Luke 11:51), the name *Barachias* perhaps being a scribal mistake.[2] Aspects of the career of Zacharias in the New Testament seem to have mirrored the experiences of both his namesakes. Like the prophet Zechariah, Zacharias was inspired of God and prophesied of the Messiah's saving mission, and, according to one postbiblical tradition, Zacharias the husband of Elisabeth was eventually martyred by wicked king Herod.[3] But in the first chapter of Luke's Infancy Narrative, the greatest comparisons and contrasts are those that Zacharias provides with Mary.

Bach's *Christmas Oratorio*

One of the undoubted masterpieces of Johann Sebastian Bach (1685–1750) is his *Christmas Oratorio*, although its length has kept it from becoming familiar to many modern listening audiences. Nevertheless, as a musical heir of Corelli and a contemporary of Handel, Bach holds an important place in the realm of great, full-length Christmas music. Written in 1734, the *Christmas Oratorio* is not an oratorio in the conventional sense but rather a set of six cantatas intended to be performed separately in the period between Christmas Day and Epiphany on January 6. While Bach often reused and adapted music that he had previously written for other works, he skillfully set some previously composed music to new Christmas texts. As with his great *St. Matthew Passion* and *St. John Passion* written for the Easter season, the biblical text is sung by a tenor narrator with interspersed chorales, choruses, and arias that draw upon poetic material.

Each of the six parts of the *Christmas Oratorio* covers a scene or story from Luke 2 and Matthew 2:

- Jesus' birth
- the angel's annunciation to the shepherds
- the adoration of the baby by the shepherds
- Jesus' presentation in the temple
- the journey of the Magi
- the Magi's adoration of Jesus

While these episodes all occur after the stories recounted in Luke 1, listening to portions of Bach's *Christmas Oratorio* at any time inevitably contributes to the Christmas spirit. Like Handel's more famous *Messiah*, this composition is a testament to the sentiment, piety, and fervor that these composers felt towards their work—and their Savior.[4]

The narrative about Zacharias and Elisabeth sets up the pattern for Mary's story that follows it. Each begins by establishing the setting and introducing the major characters (Luke 1:5–7, 26–27). An angelic visitation then follows (Luke 1:8–23, 28–38), after which Luke concludes with a scene in which each mother-to-be praises God for blessing her with a promised child (Luke 1:24–25, 39–56). Luke establishes the setting of Zacharias's story by writing, "There was in the days of Herod, the king of Judæa, a certain priest" (Luke 1:5). Proclaimed "king of the Jews" by the Roman senate in 40 B.C., Herod gained control of most of the Holy Land with Roman help in 37 B.C. and ruled it as a client ruler until his death in 4 B.C. Ethnically an Idumean hailing from the region just south of Judea, Herod's family had converted to Judaism a few generations before, and he was rarely viewed as truly Jewish by many of those whom he ruled. Further, not being from the house of David, he did not meet the messianic expectations of a legitimate ruler. Nevertheless, despite his poor reputation in most historical and Jewish sources, Herod did protect the Jewish religion, encouraging its practice and rebuilding and augmenting the temple under his rule.[5]

Wikimedia

Portrait of Zacharias and Elizabeth, *by James Tissot.*

Luke then introduces Zacharias as both a priest and as the husband of Elisabeth, who was also of the house of Aaron. Aaron's descendants were the hereditary priests of the Lord under the Mosaic order, but by the time of King David they had become so numerous that David had divided them into 24 "divisions," or courses, each of which took turns officiating in the temple (1 Chronicles 24:1–19).[6] Zacharias's course was named for Abijah or Abia, who was a descendant of Aaron's son Eleazar. While the priesthood was hereditary, Herod, like some of his predecessors before him, appointed high priests for political reasons, drawing them from families outside of the legitimate line that descended from David's and Solomon's high priest, Zadok. As a result, it is possible that a priestly family such as that of Zacharias might have had better claim to the position than the sitting high priest, explaining why

Zacharias—and his son John—might perhaps be viewed as the proper heirs of the high priesthood in their day.[7]

Both Zacharias and his wife are described as being "righteous [Greek, *dikaios*] before God, walking in all the commandments and ordinances of the Lord blameless" (Luke 1:6). Thus, like Joseph the Carpenter, who was also described as being "just" (Matthew 1:19) or "in harmony with the law," they appear in the Infancy Narrative as individuals who keep the law of Moses fully and are approved by God.[8] Luke's approbation of them in this regard is particularly striking because the author of this Gospel is usually held to be a missionary companion of the Apostle Paul (Colossians 4:14; 2 Timothy 4:11; Philemon 1:24), who in his writings stressed the virtual impossibility of keeping the law (see, for example, Romans 3:23 and Galatians 2:16).

Perhaps because of their diligence in keeping the law, Zacharias and Elisabeth were concerned by their inability to have children, because failure to conceive was sometimes seen as a sign of divine disapproval (Deuteronomy 7:14).[9] As was typical for that period and culture, their infertility was assumed to have been because of Elisabeth. By describing them not only as childless but also as being "well stricken in years," Luke creates a parallel between Zacharias and Elisabeth and Abraham and Sarah, who likewise yearned for children and then very late in life were blessed with an unexpected and miraculous conception (Genesis 18:9–15; 21:1–7). Another parallel appears in the characters of Elkanah and Hannah, who were also cured of barrenness and in return pledged that their son, Samuel, would be given to the Lord under the special conditions required of a Nazarite, which were the same conditions that were required of John (1 Samuel 1:11; Luke 1:15).[10]

After establishing this background, Luke continues with Zacharias's story by relating how he went up to the temple to serve along with the other members of his priestly course. Each of these courses served for only one week twice per year. Because of the number of priests in this period, their duties in the temple were distributed by lot. In this instance, the lot that fell to Zacharias assigned him the greatest honor, the duty to enter the holy place and offer up incense on the golden altar there, a privilege a priest could only hope for once in his life (Luke 1:9).[11] Only the high priest entered the Holy of Holies and then only once a year on the Day of Atonement. But a regular priest who drew this lot could symbolically come close to the Lord on other days by standing before the veil and offering prayer that was symbolized by the clouds of incense rising from the altar. A priest in this position represented the people, praying for the Lord's favor upon them and perhaps entreating him for deliverance, but it is natural to imagine that Zacharias had personal petitions in his heart as well.[12]

While Zacharias prayed, an angel of the Lord appeared to him, standing on the right side of the altar of incense. What happens next can be called "the annunciation to Zacharias," and it follows a pattern known as a "commissioning story," familiar from the Old Testament in which figures such as Moses and Gideon received their prophetic calls (see Exodus 3; Judges 6). In such a commissioning story, an angel appears to a prophet or other designated servant of the Lord, who expresses fear or surprise. The angel then delivers a message or call, after which the recipient reacts, often by expressing an objection. The angel then performs or gives a sign that convinces the one receiving the commission that the message is genuine and from the Lord.[13]

When the angel appears to Zacharias, in accordance with this standard commissioning pattern, the priest is at first "troubled, and fear fell upon him" (Luke 1:12). Then the angel pronounces these welcome words: "Fear not, Zacharias: for thy prayer is heard; and thy wife Elisabeth shall bear thee a son, and thou shalt name him John. And thou shalt have joy and gladness; and many shall rejoice at his birth" (Luke 1:13–14). The revealed name, *Yohanan* in Hebrew, means "God is gracious." The next angelic statement, that John's birth would bring joy, gladness, and rejoicing, serves as an anticipation of the birth of Jesus, which would be such "good tidings of great joy" for all people (Luke 2:10). Beyond these two instances of miraculous births, these statements of joy evoke the feeling that should accompany the delivery of any newborn child. As Jesus himself would later teach his disciples, "A woman when she is in travail hath sorrow, because her hour is come: but as soon as she is delivered of the child, she remembereth no more the anguish, for joy that a man is born into the world" (John 16:21). Thus, these extraordinary stories are tied to the lives and experiences of many in every age.

The angel next prophesies regarding the mission of Zacharias's promised son, noting that he shall turn "many of the children of Israel" to the Lord and, like Elijah in the prophecy of Malachi, "turn the hearts of the fathers to the children" to prepare them for the Lord (Luke 1:16–17; see also Malachi

Courtesy of Kent Jackson.

The Temple Mount today as seen from the Orson Hyde Memorial Garden on the Mount of Olives.

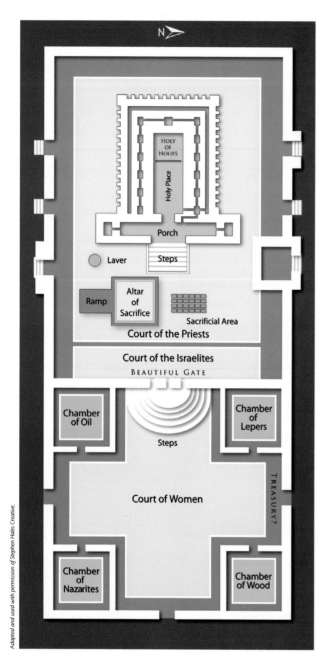

Adapted and used with permission of Stephen Holes Creative.

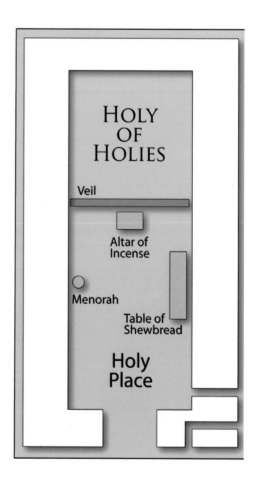

Details of the temple and its inner courts from the time of Jesus. Zacharias would have prayed alone as he made his offering before the Altar of Incense in the Holy Place.

4:5–6). Luke thus provides the background for John's mission as otherwise known from all the synoptic Gospels. Through his mission of preaching repentance, baptizing, and witnessing of the promised Messiah, John worked to prepare people for Jesus.

No doubt feeling overwhelmed by both the visionary experience he was having and the import of the news he was given, Zacharias evidences momentary uncertainty: "Whereby shall I know this? for I am an old man, and my wife well stricken in years" (Luke 1:18). The angel then identifies himself

as *Gabrî'ēl* (Luke 1:19), which in Hebrew means "the strength of God" or perhaps "man of God."[14] Known as a divine guide and informant from Daniel 8:15–16 and 9:21, Gabriel is associated in that text with eschatological, or last days, events. Latter-day revelation identifies him as the postmortal Noah, who, having been the instrument through which God preserved humanity from the flood, had a vested interest in the salvation of his descendants. By revealing the angel's name here, Luke ties Zacharias's story more closely with Mary's story that follows because the same Gabriel visits her. Here, however, Zacharias's uncertain response contrasts with Mary's, and as a result Zacharias is smitten dumb[15] as a sign or testimony not only to him but also to those outside the temple who were waiting for him to emerge and pronounce the customary blessing (Luke 1:20–22).

Zacharias's story closes with him finishing his period of service in the temple and returning to his home in the Judean countryside, where his wife conceives in accordance with the angelic pronouncement. Elisabeth concludes the episode by noting how the Lord has dealt favorably with her, taking away her reproach (Luke 1:23–25). Appropriately enough, the name *'Elîšeḇa'* generally is taken to mean "my God is the one by whom to swear," or "God is my covenant," though an alternate form can mean "my God is fortune."[16] As we reflect on the joy of this righteous woman who realizes her deepest wish after a near-lifetime of waiting, we are thus prepared for a powerful contrast: the story of a young girl who would conceive against all expectation, a story that was astonishing and, no doubt, frightening to her but which would bring joy to all the world.

Courtesy of Bridgeman Art Library; Used by permission.

Vision of Zacharias, *by James Tissot.*

MARY'S STORY

Traditionally known as the Annunciation, the story of Gabriel's visit and message to Mary (Luke 1:26–38) is one of the most celebrated of the Christmas stories. Known perhaps as well through art as from the text of Luke, the image of the Annunciation is striking. Rather than an angel appearing to an experienced priest in the temple, here the divine messenger appears to a young girl in her own village. Fewer details are known, however, than are often assumed. Although Jewish girls in this period would often become engaged in their early or mid-teens,[17] Mary's age at the time of Gabriel's appearance is not known. Nor is it known exactly where she was or what she was doing when the angel appeared to her, though works of art often depict her spinning,[18] performing other domestic tasks, or reading either within her home or sitting in a portico just outside it.[19] The Greek text states that "the angel came in [*eiselthōn*] unto her" (Luke 1:28), suggesting that she was inside somewhere. But Luke's account of Mary's story focuses only on the basic setting—who she was and what message Gabriel gave to her. Like Zacharias's, Mary's experience follows the basic steps of an Old Testament commissioning experience, but her reactions are different in critical ways.

Luke sets the scene for the Annunciation by establishing more closely the time frame in which it occurred. Whereas the annunciation to Zacharias occurred at an uncertain time "in the days of Herod, the king" (Luke 1:5), Gabriel was sent to Mary in the sixth month of Elisabeth's pregnancy. Likewise, while the home of Zacharias and Elisabeth is only later described as being somewhere in "the hill country" of Judah (Luke 1:39), Luke locates Mary specifically in "a city of Galilee, named Nazareth" (Luke 1:26).[20] In Old Testament times Galilee had been a region inhabited primarily by the tribes of Zebulun and Naphtali, but most of the inhabitants seem to have been deported by the Assyrians in 732 and 722 B.C. The region was retaken by a Jewish force under the Hasmonean king Aristobulus in 104 B.C.; those living there, both Gentiles and lapsed Israelites, were forcibly Judaized, and many Jews from the southern region of Judea were relocated there. Presumably, the ancestors of Mary's family were among these settlers. If they were of the house of David, as they seem to have been, they may have chosen the village of Nazareth because it was small and fairly obscure, and this may have helped them escape notice while the Hasmoneans and then Herodians were ruling the Holy Land.[21] Perhaps supportive of this is the possible etymology of Nazareth, which might have come from *nēṣer*, a word that can mean "branch" and might be connected with the prophecy in Isaiah 11:1 regarding a branch from the stem of Jesse. This theory suggests that the village took its name from the fact that a branch of the house of David had settled there.[22]

When Mary is first mentioned, she is identified simply as a virgin rather than by name, emphasizing her state more than her identity. As with the Greek text of Matthew 1:23, in Luke there is none of the possible ambiguity in the meaning of the term *parthenos* as there may have been with *'almâ*, the word used in the Hebrew text of Isaiah 7:14 (see Chapter 1: Son of David). She is next identified by her relationship to Joseph, who, as in Matthew, is explicitly identified as a member of the house of David.

Old Testament Figures, New Testament Saints

Although Luke is generally characterized as a Greek writing for Greeks, his Gospel nonetheless reveals a great familiarity with Jewish scripture and history. Indeed, scholars of Luke's texts often see his Gospel as serving as a bridge between the Old Testament and the New Testament Church. In what is sometimes called a "salvation history" approach, Luke seems to have viewed God's interactions with his people as occurring in three distinct phases: first, he worked through his chosen people, Israel; next, he worked through the person of his Son, Jesus; finally, after the ascension of Jesus, he began to work through Christ's Church. While the Gospel of Luke obviously represents the period of God's working directly through his Son, as the bridge between Old Testament Israel and the New Testament Church, this Gospel actually contains all three phases in its text. The Infancy Narrative (Luke 1:1–2:52) overlaps with the earlier, Old Testament period, and the Gospel's closing passage documenting Jesus' final commission to his Apostles and his ascension into heaven (Luke 24:44–53) anticipates the same stories in Luke's Book of Acts, which chronicles the rise and growth of the New Testament Church.[23]

Luke's Infancy Narrative evokes the Old Testament in many ways. On a stylistic level, in the Greek that Luke uses for these chapters he imitates the Septuagint, the Greek translation of the Old Testament.[24] Significantly, in harmony with his attention to women's stories elsewhere in his text, Luke presents his characters in the Infancy Narrative in gender pairs, with a female character matching each central male figure.[25] Thus Zacharias is matched with Elisabeth, Joseph with Mary, and Simeon with Anna, emphasizing that both men *and* women played a vital role in the coming forth of Jesus. These characters echo Old Testament prototypes, Zacharias resonating with Abraham, Elisabeth with Sarah, and both with the parents of Samson. Mary echoes several prophetic women but especially Hannah, the mother of Samuel. Finally, Simeon and Anna are prophetic figures reflecting Old Testament figures such as Isaiah and Huldah.[26] Like the Old Testament patriarchs, figures in the Infancy Narrative such as Zacharias are not always perfect, but they are nonetheless portrayed as righteous Israelites whose faith has prepared them for the roles they will play. Further, Luke's New Testament Saints are in fact prophets, moved upon by the Holy Ghost to bear witness of or to praise God.

If Joseph was also from Nazareth, his family's presence in the village might support the idea that a branch of the Davidic family had found refuge there. Yet while it is natural to assume that the man to whom Mary was betrothed or engaged lived nearby, Luke does not, in fact, say anything else about Joseph. This, together with Matthew's seeming placement of Joseph in Bethlehem from the beginning of Matthew's account, raises the possibility that he might not, in fact, have been from Nazareth himself. Many, if not most, marriages in this period were arranged, frequently among members of the same extended family and clan, which would not require the two parties to actually know each other

Courtesy of Chad Emmett.

The modern city of Nazareth from the northeast. The pointed cupola of the Church of the Annunciation appears at the right center.

personally. If Mary and Joseph were both from branches of the house of David, it is possible that one might have lived in Nazareth and the other in Bethlehem, the traditional home of David.[27]

Only after making this connection with Joseph and the house of David does Luke actually give *Mary* as the name of the virgin whom Gabriel came to visit. Appearing in Greek as both *Maria* and *Mariam,* the name in Hebrew is *Miryam,* or "Miriam," and means "height, summit, or excellence."[28] The sister of Moses, the Old Testament Miriam, is identified as having been a prophetess in a passage in which she led the women of Israel in a song praising the Lord (see Exodus 15:20–21).[29] In this she served as a model for Mary's own song of praise, but the name Miriam itself was a common one for Jewish women in the first century A.D., with at least seven different women bearing that name in the New Testament.[30] As a result, Mary herself presents an image of contrasts: betrothed to a man of the house of David and presumably from that lineage herself, she lived in a small, little-known village in Galilee. As the object of prophecy and special preparation (see the discussions of 1 Nephi 11:12–20, Mosiah 3:8, and Alma 7:10 in Chapter 5), she bore a common name shared by countless of her peers and was probably not seen as different from any of them.

As a result, Gabriel's appearance to her at the site commemorated by the Basilica of the Annunciation was unexpected.[31] Likewise surprising was the angel's unusual greeting, "Hail, thou that art highly favoured, the Lord is with thee: blessed art thou among women" (Luke 1:28). The greeting *chaire* that is translated as "hail" is a fairly standard Greek salutation, but through its Latin translation, *ave,* it has entered the Christian musical and even liturgical lexicon to reflect the honored position of Mary as the one chosen to be the mother of the Son of God. The basic meaning of *chaire* is "to rejoice" or "be glad," but it may have some connection with the Greek term *kecharitōmenē,* which the King James Version translates as "art highly favored." *Charizomai,* the root of *kecharitōmenē,* means "to find favor or do a kindness" and is a verbal form of *charis,* which means "grace," "goodwill," or, especially in the writings of Paul, "a free gift." Presumably Luke understood that this meaning in Greek parallels the meaning of the Hebrew name *Ḥannah,* which means "he [God] has favored me," and hence "grace." This connects Mary with Hannah, the mother of the prophet Samuel, who, like Miriam, is a model for Mary not only in her miraculous conception but also in her poetic, inspired song of praise.

Gabriel's appearance and greeting serve as the first part of the commission pattern that we saw with Zacharias. Like the old priest, Mary's initial reaction is to be troubled (Greek *dietarachthē,* literally "very disturbed, shaken, thrown into confusion"), but while Zacharias was distressed at the mere sight of the angel, Mary's concern is the manner of Gabriel's greeting, wondering "what manner of salutation this should be" (Luke 1:29). As with Zacharias, the angel first tells her to not be afraid and again emphasizes that she had "found favor [*charin* or "grace"] with God," after which he delivers his message: "And, behold, thou shalt conceive in thy womb, and bring forth a son, and shalt call his name Jesus. He shall be great, and shall be called the Son of the Highest: and the Lord God shall give unto him the throne of his father David; and he shall reign over the house of Jacob for ever; and of his kingdom there shall be no end" (Luke 1:31–33). As with the annunciation to Joseph, here the angel directs that the child be named *Yəhôšûa* or "YHWH saves." But while the emphasis in Matthew's account was on Joseph's role as the legal father or guardian of Jesus, thus making him the Son of David, in Luke's story Jesus is first and foremost "the Son of the Highest," though he will also inherit the throne of his father David.

Following the commission pattern, Mary reacts, but rather than wondering how she could know whether the angel's message was true, she simply wonders, "How shall this be, seeing I know not a man?" (Luke 1:34). In other words, Zacharias, given his and his wife's age, wanted a sign that John's birth *would* happen, but Mary innocently wanted to know *how* it could occur. To this question, the angel responds with

A modern Christian Arab couple celebrates their wedding in Nazareth.

the amazing pronouncement, "The Holy Ghost shall come upon thee, and the power of the Highest shall overshadow thee: therefore also that holy thing which shall be born of thee shall be called the Son of God" (Luke 1:35). As with Matthew 1:18 and 20, *pneuma hagion,* rendered in the King James Version as "*the* Holy Ghost," lacks the definite article "the" in the Greek text.[32] This suggests that it was the holy power of God, or the actual spirit of God—which is

The Annunciation, *by John William Waterhouse.*

parallel here with "the power of the Highest" overshadowing her in the next phrase—that would be the agent that was to bring about this divine conception (see the discussion of Alma 7:10 in Chapter 5). Nevertheless, more than the mere power of God is suggested here: the Greek term *episkiasei,* translated "overshadow," is used by the Septuagint in Exodus 40:35 for the presence of God himself that rested upon the Tabernacle.[33] Whereas the conception of John was miraculous, it was otherwise the natural result of relations between a married man and his wife. The conception of Jesus, however, was both miraculous and divine.[34]

While Mary does not ask for a sign in the way that Zacharias or others in the commissioning pattern sometimes did, Gabriel nonetheless provides her with one: Elisabeth, Mary's relative (Greek, *syngenis;* KJV, "cousin") has conceived even though she had been called barren. He explains that with God nothing is impossible, to which Mary meekly responds, "Behold the handmaid of the Lord; be it unto me according to thy word" (Luke 1:38). With this simple affirmation of faith and obedience, Mary accepts her exalted call to become the mother of the Son of God. Nothing more is said in the account of either Matthew or Luke as to how this conception occurred other than that it was by the power of God. However this was brought about, Nephi maintains that she was still a virgin even after she brought forth her firstborn son (see 1 Nephi 11:20). President Harold B. Lee counseled: "If teachers were wise in speaking of this matter about which the Lord has said but very little, they would rest their discussion on this subject with merely the words which are recorded on this subject in Luke 1:34–35. . . . Remember that the being who was brought about by Mary's conception was a divine personage. We need not question His method to accomplish His purposes."[35]

MARY VISITS ELISABETH

With the angel's revelation that Elisabeth was pregnant, Mary made the journey of some 100 miles to Judea to visit her kinswoman in an episode traditionally known as the Visitation (Luke 1:39–56). Although the exact location of Zacharias and Elisabeth's home in the hill country of Judea is not known, since the sixth century it has traditionally been identified with the site of the village of En Kerem, just west of Jerusalem.[36] Luke does not give any details of Mary's trip, but it is unlikely that a young woman in this period could have made the journey alone or without her parents' knowledge. Because the Greek term *syngenis* simply means "kinswoman" and does not necessarily indicate whether they were first cousins or more distant relatives, we cannot speculate much on their relationship, though it seems probable that Mary knew her relative and was comfortable traveling to see and then stay with her. Putting the two women together provides Luke with a further opportunity to compare and contrast the stories of the conceptions of both John and Jesus.

Neither Mary nor Elisabeth would have known of the other's condition without revelation. Luke 1:24–25 records that Elisabeth had gone into confinement as soon as she conceived, keeping herself hidden for five months until the sixth month, when Gabriel revealed the pregnancy to Mary. Likewise, Mary's own new pregnancy would probably not have been apparent when she arrived at Zacharias's home. However, just as the angel informed Mary of Elisabeth's good news, the Spirit informs Elisabeth of Mary's

Courtesy of Kent Jackson

The current Basilica of the Annunciation is a Roman Catholic church built in 1969 on the site of earlier Byzantine and Crusader churches. All of these were built on the spot purported to be Mary's home.

Hört zu ihr lieben Leute
"O Hear Ye, Good People"

Luke's account of the Annunciation has provided inspiration to artists and musicians alike. Michael Praetorius (1571–1621), a prolific German composer and musical scholar, provided a beautiful musical setting for this scene when he adapted a motet—or song based on a sacred text written for different voices—that had been written shortly before by Daniel Rumpius. Rumpius drew his text from Luke 1:28–31, arranging it in alternating German and Latin text, thereby connecting it with earlier traditions of sacred music. Although the four stanzas reproduced below are the most familiar, the original lyrics stretched to eighteen verses. While each verse had different German text, the Latin lines repeated in every stanza, so here they appear in Latin in the first verse but in italicized English in the last three.[37]

O all ye people, give ear,
Ecce mundi gaudia.
The story of God's birth to hear,
Summa cum laetitia.
O virgo Maria,
Es plena gratia.

He greeted there a pure maid;
Behold joy of the world,
He found her alone as she prayed,
With greatest sadness
O virgin Mary
You are full of grace.

The angel Gabriel flew down,
Behold joy of the world,
At God's command, to Naz'reth town,
With greatest gladness
O virgin Mary
You are full of grace.

He said, "Hail Mary
Behold joy of the world,
Thou, thou a holy son shall bear,
With greatest gladness."
O virgin Mary
You are full of grace.

Praetorius was a pivotal musical figure, bringing Italian performance practices to Germany while serving as an important innovator in Protestant church music. As such, he was a forerunner of Handel, and his music makes beautiful listening at any season of the year. But when approaching Christmastime, his arrangement of *Hört zu ihr lieben Leute* recreates the scene of the Annunciation while tying together Medieval, Renaissance, and Baroque music.

The Greek Orthodox Church of the Annunciation sits on another site, over the spring where tradition holds Mary was drawing water when the angel Gabriel appeared to her.

miracle. Responding immediately to the presence of Mary and the yet unborn Jesus, John, still in the womb, leaps with joy, and Elisabeth is filled with the Spirit (Luke 1:40–42, 44). The angel had told Zacharias that his son would "be filled with the Holy Ghost, even from his mother's womb" (Luke 1:15), and this first prophetic act recognizing the promised Savior helps explain why Jesus would later say, "Among them that are born of women there hath not risen a greater [prophet] than John the Baptist" (Matthew 11:11).

Functioning in an inspired role herself, Elisabeth utters a brief, poetic expression that begins, "Blessed art thou among women, and blessed is the fruit of thy womb" (Luke 1:42).[38] In an interesting contrast with her own husband, who was unable to pronounce the required blessing as he came out of the temple, this faithful woman is able to bless both Mary and the unborn Jesus, recognizing the latter as her Lord. By concluding "blessed is she that believed: for there shall be a performance of those things which were told her from the Lord" (Luke 1:45), Elisabeth may be continuing the contrast with Zacharias, who seems not to have believed at first. But more importantly, she invokes a blessing on both herself and Mary, both of whom trusted in the Lord's promises to them.[39]

Elisabeth's inspired expression anticipates Mary's own poetic response. Traditionally known as the *Magnificat,* from the first word in its Latin translation (*magnificat anima mea Dominum*), it is the first of the canticles, or religious songs, that Luke weaves into his Infancy Narrative. Like other canticles, this one draws upon the rich tradition of Old Testament poetry, applying earlier motifs to specific New Testament situations. Thus Mary's canticle has much in common with the heartfelt song of Hannah (see 1 Samuel 2:1–10),[40] but the implications are far greater. The *Magnificat* can be divided into four sections or stanzas, the first of which is an introductory expression of praise: "My soul doth magnify the Lord, and my spirit hath rejoiced in God my Saviour" (Luke 1:46–47). Mary's words resonate with similar Old Testament expressions (see 1 Samuel 2:1–2; Psalm 33:5; Habakkuk 3:18), but the phrases here find singular application, attesting Mary's role in glorifying and helping bring about the purposes of the Lord while she rejoices not only in the Lord in terms of general salvation but also that Jesus will be *the* Savior. The second stanza then focuses on what God has done for Mary, recalling how he has regarded her low estate and done great things, leading all generations to call her blessed (Luke 1:48–49). The third section contrasts those who fear God with those who are proud (Luke 1:50–53; 1 Samuel

Courtesy of Chad Emmett.

Ein Kerem, *which means "spring of the vineyard," is a town just southwest of Jerusalem that Christian tradition holds was the home of Zacharias and Elisabeth.*

2:4–8; Job 12:19; Psalm 89:11, 107:9; Ezekiel 21:31), showing how God will triumph over the god-less, much as Miriam's song celebrated the Lord's victory over the Egyptians at the Red Sea (Exodus 15:1–8).[41] The final stanza concludes by proclaiming what God has done—and will do—for Israel. Noting that God has remembered his people and has been merciful to her, Mary's song connects the mission of her Son to the covenants that God made with Abraham and David (Luke 1:54–55; see 2 Samuel 22:51; Psalm 98:3; Isaiah 41:8–9; Micah 7:20).

The *Magnificat* dominates the account of the Visitation, suggesting that its important themes of mercy, salvation, and covenant-keeping are far greater and more universal than the experiences of Mary and Elisabeth. Its effect, however, is to personalize the scene, giving us as readers a sense of Mary as a real person and drawing us into her experience. Having succeeded both in dramatizing the episode and weaving gospel themes into it, Luke then succinctly concludes without giving any more details of the experiences of the women together. He simply notes that after three months, just shortly before Elisabeth gave birth, Mary returned to her own home (Luke 1:56). Nevertheless, Luke's account of Mary's visit to Elisabeth provides us with the stirring image of two faithful and inspired women who, like Sarah, Miriam, and Hannah before them, rely upon the promises of the Lord and are inspired in praising him.

THE BIRTH OF JOHN THE BAPTIST

The final scene in Luke 1 is the birth and blessing of John the Baptist (Luke 1:57–80). It anticipates and also contrasts with the story of Jesus' own birth and blessing in Luke 2. In this scene, John's birth is reported briefly, with more attention given to his circumcision and naming; in Luke 2, the events surrounding Jesus' birth are extensively described, while the circumcision and naming take but one verse (Luke 2:21).[42] The story of John's birth begins after Mary's departure, with Luke noting that Elisabeth's pregnancy came to full term and that she brought forth a son, which caused her neighbors and relatives to rejoice with her as they recognized the great mercy that the Lord had shown her (Luke 1:57–58). In her own home, surrounded by family and friends, Elisabeth and her experience with her firstborn son provide a contrast to the story of Mary's experience, which will be away from home and, seemingly, only attended by strangers.

Mary's Visit to Elizabeth, *by Frans Francken.*

As was customary, friends and family gathered at Zacharias and Elisabeth's home on the occasion of their son's circumcision and naming. Those who had gathered proposed that the baby be named after his father, Zacharias. Elisabeth, who had learned of the angelic instruction to her husband, insisted that he would instead be named John, which, as we have noted, means "God is gracious." The Lord had indeed been gracious to the old couple, and when Zacharias acknowledged this by writing that the child's name would be John, he was freed of the sign of dumbness which apparently had been imposed upon him for unbelief. This, too, was seen as a miracle, and news of it spread around the hill country of Judea, causing people to wonder, "What manner of child shall this be!" (Luke 1:66).

Zacharias, filled with the Holy Ghost as Mary and Elisabeth had

The Canticles in Luke

Whereas Matthew's Infancy Narrative is characterized by his frequent use of Old Testament scripture, Luke's is distinctive for his use of poetic interludes that his central figures utter at pivotal points in the story. These are generally known as canticles, a word which comes from the Latin diminutive term *canticulum*, meaning "song." The term is generally used in some churches' liturgies for any religious song taken from a biblical passage, usually from Old Testament books other than Psalms. The name is also applied to four passages in Luke's Infancy Narrative that are known by traditional Latin titles that reflect their opening lines: the *Magnificat* (Mary, "My soul doth *magnify* the Lord," Luke 1:46–55; emphasis added), the *Benedictus*

Courtesy of Bridgeman Art Library. Used by permission.

The Magnificat, *by James Tissot.*

(Zacharias, "*Blessed* be the Lord God of Israel," Luke 1:68–79; emphasis added), the *Gloria in Excelsis* (the angels, "*Glory to God in the Highest*," Luke 2:14; emphasis added), and the *Nunc Demittis* (Simeon, "Lord, *now lettest thou thy servant depart* in peace," Luke 2:29–32; emphasis added).

Although Luke wrote in Greek—and indeed, elsewhere in his Gospel and the book of Acts, his writings are the most literary Greek in the New Testament—the canticles reflect significant Semitic influence, meaning that they reveal Hebrew or Aramaic influences or prototypes behind the Greek text. This, together with the question of how Luke could have known the exact words that characters uttered at those particular moments, has raised important compositional questions. What were Luke's sources? Did he translate verbatim reports of the songs of Mary, Zacharias, the angels, and Simeon that were somehow reported to him, or did he exercise creative license in crafting the canticles as they now appear? Further, all of the canticles echo important Old Testament passages, suggesting that the original speakers, Luke's sources, or Luke himself knew these passages and applied them to the situations that Luke describes.

Many scholars suggest that the canticles were preexisting Hebrew songs that Luke translated and adapted to his story. Their theory comes from observing that the canticles interrupt the context of the narrative, use different vocabulary than the surrounding text, exhibit a poetic style that is more Hebrew than Greek, and sometimes seem to be only loosely connected to the story that Luke is telling. This theory suggests that themes of deliverance and God's coming salvation would have been common in the first century, and Jewish groups could have used Old Testament scripture to craft prayers or songs.[43] While this is possible, it is just as likely that those whom Luke describes, all righteous Israelites, would have known the same scriptural passages and had those same aspirations and hopes. As a result, the basic sense of the canticles could have originated with the characters themselves, even if their utterances were subsequently rephrased and even elaborated upon as they were retold by early Christians, becoming the Hebrew or Aramaic sources for Luke who then translated them into Greek.

Regardless of their compositional history, the canticles as we have them today play an important and powerful role in Luke's narrative. They effectively illustrate the feelings of those involved, draw the reader into the story, and movingly teach broader doctrine. Like Matthew's formula quotations, Luke's canticles connect his story with the Old Testament past and draw upon its promises. Clearly inspired, they witness that the same spirit which moved the original Old Testament authors likewise filled the figures involved, the early Christians who passed along their stories, and Luke himself as he wrote those stories down.

Courtesy of Chad Emmett.

Rebuilt over the course of the last several hundred years, the Church of the Visitation marks the spot where Mary visited her relative Elisabeth and where she recited the Magnificat canticle. The text to this song appears in many languages on tiles throughout the church.

been earlier, prophesied regarding both God's goodness and the future mission of his son. Luke presents this prophecy as the second of his canticles, known traditionally as the *Benedictus,* the Latin translation of its first word, "blessed" (Luke 1:68–79). The song of Zacharias divides into three stanzas, only the last of which deals directly with the situation immediately at hand. Instead, the first stanza deals with the deliverance that will come through the promised Savior of the house of David (Luke 1:68–71). This stanza begins in customary Hebrew fashion by first blessing God. Then, echoing several Old Testament passages, it proceeds to describe how he has visited, redeemed, and saved his people by raising up a "horn," or "source of strength," for Israel in the house of David, as had been prophesied from the beginning (see Judges 3:9; Psalm 18:2, 17; 111:9). The next section focuses on the covenant which God made with Abraham, promising that his seed would be granted mercy and deliverance to serve God in holiness and righteousness (Luke 1:72–77; see Exodus

Blessing and Magnifying the Lord

When Zacharias emerged from the temple after his vision of the angel Gabriel, he was not able to pronounce the expected priestly benediction, or blessing: "The Lord bless thee, and keep thee: the Lord make his face shine upon thee, and be gracious unto thee: the Lord lift up his countenance upon thee, and give thee peace" (Numbers 6:24–26). On the other hand, Elisabeth, upon meeting Mary, immediately blessed the mother of her Lord. She then proclaims, "blessed is she that believed" (Luke 1:45), which can be taken to include herself, certainly Mary, and by extension all faithful women who trust in the promises that God makes to them. Only upon fulfilling the angel's direction to name his promised son John was Zacharias's tongue loosed, whereupon he did not begin by blessing his son or others but by first blessing God. This is in harmony with Jewish practice, in which many prayers begin not by asking for blessings for others but by pronouncing the Lord himself as "blessed" because of his goodness, recognizing that he is the source of all our blessings. The implication is important for us—if we fail to trust God and his promises, we may not be able to bless others or obtain blessings for ourselves. However, if we see him as the source of all blessings and recognize his hand in our lives, we can realize his promises and be empowered to bless the lives of others.

Mary, who stands as the preeminent example in Luke's account of one who both trusted the Lord and was blessed by him, begins her song with the interesting phrase, "My soul doth *magnify* the Lord" (Luke 1:46; emphasis added). The Greek verb *megalunei*, which means "to make great" and "to extol, to praise," was rendered in Latin with the verb *magnificat*, from which we get the English "magnify." This word produces interesting connotations, particularly for Latter-day Saints, who frequently speak of "magnifying our callings," or fulfilling our responsibilities. Mary praised the Lord and rejoiced in God because she saw him as the source of goodness and, in her case, as the real agent in bringing forth the promised Savior. For us to magnify the Lord, we, too, must recognize God as the source of all blessings, trust in his promises, and above all, do our part in helping bring Jesus more fully into the world. As Mary filled her exalted role by becoming the mother of Jesus in the flesh, so can we fulfill our calling and greatly bless others by standing as a witness of our Savior "at all times and in all things, and in all places" (Mosiah 18:9).

2:24; Psalm 89:4; Isaiah 38:20; Micah 7:20). By focusing on these two Old Testament figures, David and Abraham, Zacharias's song effectively establishes the same connections that Matthew's genealogy does.[44] Only in the last stanza does Zacharias's song, or prophecy, treat the mission of the baby John (Luke 1:76–79). Probably the kernel of Zacharias's original blessing to his son, it too draws upon Old Testament passages, especially from the prophecies of Isaiah, to anticipate what the child would accomplish as the forerunner of Jesus (see Numbers 24:17; Isaiah 9:2; 42:6–7; 60:1).

Luke's vignette of John's birth and blessing closes with words that echo at the closing of his later description of Jesus' birth and blessing in Luke 2: "And the child *grew, and waxed strong in spirit,* and

Es ist ein Ros entsprungen
"Lo, How a Rose E'er Blooming"

Based upon Isaiah 11:1, the German poem which served as the text for this hauntingly beautiful carol was first published in 1599. In the medieval period, the family of David's father, Jesse, was often portrayed as a rose tree. Thus in this carol, Isaiah's prophecy of a rod coming forth from the stem of David's father, Jesse, and a branch out of his root is portrayed as a beautiful rose blooming. Catholics frequently saw Mary, through whom Jesus came, as that rose. After the Reformation, Protestants usually saw Christ himself as the rose.[45]

The familiar musical setting was arranged by Michael Praetorius in 1609, and Theodore Baker produced the most common English translation in 1894.[46] Regardless of whether one ascribes the role of rose to Mary or to Christ in the song, Mary's part in Jesus' arrival began with the Annunciation and was celebrated in the *Magnificat*, making this a beautiful song to associate with Luke 1.

Lo, how a Rose e'er blooming
From tender stem hath sprung!
Of Jesse's lineage coming,
As men of old have sung.

It came, a floweret bright,
Amid the cold of winter,
When half-spent was the night.

Isaiah 'twas foretold it,
The Rose I have in mind,
With Mary we behold it,
The Virgin Mother kind.

To show God's love aright,
She bore to men a Saviour
When half-spent was the night.

This Flower, whose fragrance tender
With sweetness fills the air,
Dispels with glorious splendor
The darkness everywhere.

True man, yet very God;
From sin and death He saves us,
And lightens every load.[47]

was in the deserts till the day of his shewing unto Israel" (Luke 1:80; emphasis added; see also Luke 2:40). In the stories of Zacharias, Elisabeth, and Mary, Luke provides us with models of faithfulness that complement Matthew's portrait of Joseph. All of these stories tell of men and women who accept their missions, even if they seem to, as in Zacharias's case, momentarily doubt. Responsive to revelations and the promptings of the Spirit, they are all prophetic figures who also show us how to respond to calls, challenges, and blessings that the Lord presents to us in our lives. But above all, the story of the miraculous conception and birth of the baby of Zacharias and Elisabeth stands as a foil for that of Jesus. With the comparisons and contrasts for these two stories established, Luke thus prepares his readers for the birth of the promised Savior, one of the most joyful stories ever told. ❖

THE ADVENT THEME OF LOVE

Love infuses Luke's narrative in the first chapter of his Gospel. Implicit in the story of Zacharias and Elisabeth is their love for each other. The miracle of human conception and birth underlies their story as well as Mary's, reminding us of the love that parents have for their children. Further, these three characters, and Joseph from Matthew 1, exhibit great love for the Lord, trusting in his promises and showing a willingness to be obedient to his commands. But above all, interwoven into their stories is God's great love for them and for all humanity. Indeed, this love, which is one of the greatest of all the gifts of God, underlies the entire story of Jesus' birth, sacrifice, and Resurrection, because God so loved the world that he sent his Only Begotten Son (see 1 Nephi 11:22; John 3:16–17). This love was not only manifest at Jesus' birth and through his atoning sacrifice; it can and should be present in our lives now, and it will fill the world with his return when he establishes his millennial reign, ruling with love as King of Kings and Lord of Lords.

Two of the purple candles are lit on the second Sunday of Advent, which celebrates the love of Jesus.

The second candle of an Advent wreath can be used to celebrate this love that God has shared with us in the person of his Son, Jesus. This love is also found in Christ's love for us. Indeed, God calls upon us to share this pure love of Christ—or charity (see Moroni 7:47–48)—with others not only at Christmastime but always. Some of our favorite passages about the love of God include the following:

"Sing, O heavens; and be joyful, O earth; and break forth into singing, O mountains: for the Lord hath comforted his people, and will have mercy upon his afflicted. But Zion said, The Lord hath forsaken me, and my Lord hath forgotten me. *Can a woman forget her sucking child, that she should not have compassion on the son of her womb? yea, they may forget, yet will I not forget thee.* Behold, I have graven thee upon the palms of my hands" (Isaiah 49:13–16; emphasis added).

"And it came to pass that I saw the heavens open; and an angel came down and stood before me; and he said unto me: Nephi, what beholdest thou? And I said unto him: A virgin, most beautiful and fair above all other virgins . . . And he said unto me: Behold, the virgin whom thou seest is the mother of the Son of God, after the manner of the flesh . . . And I looked and beheld the virgin again, bearing a child in her arms. And the angel said unto me: *Behold the Lamb of God, yea, even the Son of the Eternal Father!* Knowest thou the meaning of the tree which thy father saw? And I answered him, saying: Yea, *it is the love of God, which sheddeth itself abroad in the hearts of the children of men; wherefore, it is the most desirable above all things*" (1 Nephi 11:14–22; emphasis added).

"*For God so loved the world, that he gave his only begotten Son,* that whosoever believeth in him should not perish, but have everlasting life. For God sent not his Son into the world to condemn the world; but that the world through him might be saved" (John 3:16–17; emphasis added).

"But *charity is the pure love of Christ*, and it endureth forever . . . wherefore, my beloved brethren, *pray unto the Father with all the energy of heart, that ye may be filled with this love*, which he hath bestowed upon all who are true followers of his Son, Jesus Christ" (Moroni 7:47–48; emphasis added).

Just as the first Advent candle can be used to teach our children about the covenants which God made with the earliest patriarchs, we use the lighting of the second candle as an opportunity to recall as a family the great covenant that God made with Abraham, which both Mary and Zacharias recalled in their songs. The Lord assured Abraham of eternal glory and seed as numerous as the sands of the sea and further promised that in his seed all the nations of the earth would be blessed, a promise that received its ultimate fulfillment in the coming of Jesus Christ through Abraham's line.

Samuel and Rachel making Christmas cookies as part of our celebrations leading up to Christmas.

A variety of carols recalling the love and adoration that we feel toward God and his Son can be sung as part of a family celebration of Advent. Though neither of these is strictly an Advent carol, two of our favorites are "O Come, All Ye Faithful" and "O Holy Night" because they place us, symbolically, with the shepherds and others who adored the baby King at his birth. Although the exact origins of the text of "O Come, All Ye Faithful" and its tune are uncertain, the earliest Latin text, *Adeste fideles*, is attributed to John Francis Wade, an English Catholic who wrote it about 1742. Frederick Oakley translated the lyrics twice, once in 1841 and again in 1852, with his second effort becoming the standard version.[1] Oakley's English text had four verses, although the second verse does not appear in LDS hymnals. We like to sing this carol on the second Sunday of Advent because its chorus, which repeats the phrase "Oh, come, let us adore him," reflects the love that we feel for Jesus.

"O Holy Night" similarly reflects the theme of adoration with its refrain that begins with "fall on your knees." Originally a French song with words by Placide Cappeau (1808–77) and a musical setting by Adolphe Adam (1803–56), its title in that language is *Cantique de Noël* or *Minuit, Chrétiens*. In addition to the adoration expressed in its repeated chorus, "O Holy Night" also accords well with the Advent theme of love in its final verse:

> Truly He taught us to love one another,
> His law is love and His gospel is peace.
> Chains shall He break for the slave is our brother,
> And in His name all oppression shall cease.
> Sweet hymns of joy in grateful chorus raise we,
> Let all within us praise His holy name.[2]

3
BABE OF BETHLEHEM

Luke 2

And so it was, that, while they were there, the days were accomplished that she should
be delivered. And she brought forth her firstborn son, and wrapped him in swaddling clothes,
and laid him in a manger; because there was no room for them in the inn.

—Luke 2:6–7

Of all the Christmas stories in the biblical accounts of Jesus' divine conception and miraculous birth, the first two episodes in the second chapter of Luke—the story of Jesus' birth and the announcement of it to the shepherds—are without a doubt the most familiar. Each Christmas Eve countless families turn to the first half of Luke 2 to commemorate the birth of the Babe of Bethlehem, and whether alone or with loved ones, reading these stories warms our hearts as we read of "good tidings of great joy" (Luke 2:10).

These stories represent a significant expansion upon Matthew's simple notice, "she had brought forth her firstborn son: and [Joseph] called his name Jesus" (Matthew 1:25). But they are also a culmination of all that preceded in Luke's Infancy Narrative and are best understood in reference not just to Luke 1, but also to what follows in the later episodes of Luke 2. Here, Luke provides historical details not recorded elsewhere, and while making clear who Jesus was, he gives added testimony as to what he had come to do.[1]

THE TIME AND PLACE OF JESUS' BIRTH

In the tradition of classical historiography, Luke begins his account of the birth of Jesus by attempting to date it and then carefully describing the setting. While he set the conceptions of both John and Jesus in a Jewish context—"in the days of Herod, the king of Judæa" (Luke 1:5), a date and a place likewise provided by Matthew (see Matthew 2:1)—Luke places Jesus' birth on a world stage by referring to Caesar

The Holy Night, by Carl Bloch.
Courtesy Hope Gallery.

Episodes of Luke 2

- The Birth of Jesus (Luke 2:1–7)
- The Annunciation to the Shepherds (Luke 2:8–14)
  - Canticle: *Gloria in Excelsis* (Luke 2:14)
- The Adoration of the Shepherds (Luke 2:15–20)
- Naming, Purification, and Presentation (Luke 2:21–40)
  - Canticle: *Nunc Demittis* (Luke 2:29–32)
- The Boy in the Temple (Luke 2:41–52; see Conclusion: Remembering Christmas)

Crowds fill Manger Square in Bethlehem to celebrate Christmas Eve.

Augustus. The first Roman emperor, Imperator Caesar August, as he was officially known, gained control of the Roman empire and hence most of the Mediterranean world, including Judea in 31 B.C., and ruled officially as Rome's first citizen from 27 B.C. to A.D. 14. His reign thus overlapped with the first half of Jesus' life, and Luke clearly saw him in contrast to Jesus. The adopted heir of Julius Caesar, who had been deified after his death, Augustus bore the title *Divi filius,* or "son of God." Having brought more than a century of Roman civil wars to a close, the emperor reestablished peace and prosperity to the Roman world in what was called the *Pax Augusta,* or "Augustan Peace." As a result, throughout the Greek East, Augustus was frequently acclaimed as *Sōtēr,* or "Savior."[2] In contrast to this worldly political ruler, however, Luke presents Jesus as the true Son of God, the Prince of Peace, and the Savior of the world.[3]

Within the period of the reign of Augustus, Luke endeavors to date the birth of Jesus more closely by noting, "And it came to pass in those days, that there went out a decree from Caesar Augustus, *that all the world should be taxed*" (Luke 2:1; emphasis added). "All the world" is a rendering of the Greek expression *pasan tēn oikoumenēn,* which in the Hellenistic period had come to mean the entire "civilized" (e.g., Greek) world, but by Roman times meant those lands under the control of the empire. "Should be taxed" is the English translation of *apographesthai,* which actually means "be enrolled" and is probably a reference to a census and property evaluation done in advance of taxation. Luke then identifies this enrollment and registration by writing, "And this taxing [Greek, *apographē*] was *first* made *when Cyrenius was governor of Syria*" (Luke 2:2; emphasis added). Despite Luke's apparent precision, this dating actually presents a historical problem. Sources from the period establish that the governorship of Cyrenius, whose Roman name was Publius Sulpicius Quirinius, began in A.D. 6, but the date of Herod's death was 4 B.C., some ten years earlier. That Jesus' birth was, in fact, in the last years or months of Herod's reign and not during Quirinius' governorship is established not only in Matthew 2:1 and Luke 1:5 but also by Luke's date references in Luke 3:1–3, which begin the story of John's baptizing of Jesus.

A variety of proposals have been made to support the dates in Luke's Infancy Narrative. Some of these revolve around the word *first* (Greek, *prōtos*) in the phrase "this taxing was first made." Noting that it might be possible to translate this as "earlier than," or "first of several," commentators suggest that Quirinius may have been responsible for an earlier census and property evaluation besides the historically known one in A.D. 6. Another approach is to render *prōtos* as "before," resulting in the translation "this enrollment [took place] *before* Quirinius was governor." However, an added difficulty arises because, while records exist of censuses of Roman citizens and also Roman subjects in the provinces, there is no record of a universal census of the entire Roman empire. Another problem exists—Herod's kingdom at this point was a client state, allied closely with and certainly subordinate to Rome, yet still technically independent. Herod was a king within his own realm, setting and collecting his own taxes, even if he did pay tribute to Rome.[4]

Nevertheless, the lack of historical documentation does not mean that this registration or taxation did not happen. As one observer has noted, we should carefully avoid "too easy acceptance of the conclusion that Luke has gone astray here; only the discovery of new historical evidence can lead to a solution of the problem."[5] It is possible, for instance, that Herod instituted a census of his own kingdom along the lines of what was occurring elsewhere in the empire. Another possibility is that Luke might have mistakenly associated some kind of taxing at Christ's birth with a memory of the census that did occur when Judea and other portions of the Herodian kingdom became a Roman province in A.D. 6, when Herod's son and successor, Archelaus, was deposed.[6] As we wait for new documents to surface that might help resolve this question, it is more useful to understand what Luke tries to accomplish with his reference to the census. In addition to providing a comparison to and a contrast with Augustus, putting the story of Jesus in a worldwide context, Luke also uses the census to explain how and why Mary, a virgin from Nazareth in Galilee, was in Bethlehem at the time of Jesus' birth.

Regardless of who ordered the census or exactly when it was held, Luke seems to suggest that its requirements obligated both Joseph and Mary to be present in Joseph's ancestral city. While the expression "city of David" is most often applied to Jerusalem, David's later capital, David's original home was Bethlehem (see 1 Samuel 16:1–13; 20:6, 28–29), which Luke emphasizes by saying that Joseph went "unto the city of David, which is called Bethlehem; (because he was of the house and lineage of David:)" (Luke 2:4).[7] While suggestions that such a registration in one's ancestral city was done in accordance

Handel's *Messiah*

The great oratorio *Messiah*, by George Frideric Handel (1685–1759), treats the entire messianic career of Jesus Christ, beginning with prophecies of his coming and continuing through his birth, Passion, Resurrection, ascension, and promised return. Handel's collaborator Charles Jennens (1700–1773) drew the text from Old and New Testament passages, after which Handel composed the score within a few months in the summer of 1741. First performed on April 13, 1742, in Dublin, Ireland, *Messiah* was not well-received initially because some in the religious establishment did not feel that the Bible's words should be sung as entertainment. Repeated performances, however, led to wide acceptance, and it has since been generally acknowledged as one of the great pieces of musical literature.

Messiah is divided into three parts, only the first of which treats the promised birth of Jesus. The work as a whole was originally performed during Lent, the preparatory period leading up to Easter. However, it has become traditional to perform the first part together with the "Hallelujah" chorus from the second part during Advent, making it an important musical fixture of the Christmas season.[8] The first half of the section usually performed at Christmastime treats the prophecies of Jesus' coming, culminating with the chorus "For unto Us a Child Is Born," a musical setting of Isaiah 9:6. After the beautiful *Pastoral Symphony*, which is the successor of the Largo, or pastoral movement, of Corelli's *Christmas Concerto*, Handel wrote four soprano recitatives that set the text of Luke 2:8–13, recounting the angelic annunciation of Christ's birth to the shepherds. These are immediately followed by "Glory to God," a wonderful choral setting of the canticle of the angels found in Luke 2:14. Together these movements constitute a moving musical testimony of the story of Jesus' birth.

with either Jewish or regional practice are not well-supported,[9] it is possible that Joseph or his extended family had holdings in Judea because heads of households usually registered where they owned property. This requirement would generally not demand that a man's wife be present, leading some to suggest that either Joseph did not want to be separated from his wife so close to the birth of her firstborn child or that Mary also (who, we have seen, may have been of the house of David) owned property in that area and needed to register there.[10] In either case, the couple's compliance reveals that not only were they righteous Israelites who kept the law of Moses but also that they were law-abiding subjects to temporal authority.[11] Another possibility, suggested by Matthew's account, is that Joseph was from Bethlehem all along, while Mary, perhaps a relative, lived in Nazareth. If their marriage had been arranged, with the betrothal occurring when they were much younger, Joseph may have "found that she was with child" when he went to Nazareth to bring his new bride home to Bethlehem. Luke, not aware of this, may have used a misplaced memory of a later census to explain the couple's movement from Galilee to Judea.

Luke does not record any details of the journey, which could have followed one of two possible courses. One, seemingly more direct, would have taken them from Nazareth across the Jezreel Valley

Courtesy of Kent Jackson.

The central nave of the Church of the Nativity, which the Roman emperor Justinian built in A.D. 565 to replace an earlier church built by Helena, the mother of the emperor Constantine, between A.D. 327 and 333.

and then due south through Samaria. This route, however, is more circuitous than it appears on a map because of the hilly terrain, and it would also have taken them through the unfriendly country of the Samaritans. The other possibility would have been to follow the Jezreel Valley southeast until it joined the Jordan Valley, after which Joseph and Mary would have needed to ascend from Jericho through the Judean desert of Jordan to Jerusalem and then on to Bethlehem. Both routes are about ninety-two miles long and would have taken four or five days to walk.[12] While the traditional assumption that the pregnant Mary rode a donkey is possible and nicely anticipates Jesus' later Triumphal Entry into Jerusalem on a donkey, Luke does not indicate this. Most travelers, if they had an animal, would have used it to carry their baggage. In any event, the journey would have been difficult for Mary.

Regardless of external circumstances, as Joseph McConkie has suggested, "it was not the payment of taxes that brought Joseph and Mary from Nazareth to Bethlehem. . . . Mary and Joseph came from Nazareth to Bethlehem because they knew that in the providence of heaven the Christ child was to be born in Bethlehem, which was the original family home for them both."[13] Bethlehem, the name of which means "house of bread," was a peculiarly appropriate place for the birth of the child who was "the bread come down from heaven" and "the bread of life" (John 6:31–35, 41, 48, 50–51).

MARY BRINGS FORTH HER FIRSTBORN SON

In one of the most familiar verses from the Christmas story, Luke records that "she brought forth her firstborn son, and wrapped him in swaddling clothes, and laid him in a manger; because there

Courtesy of Kent Jackson.

This simple dirt road between Nazareth and Bethlehem conjures up images of Joseph and Mary's journey before that first Christmas.

was no room for them in the inn" (Luke 2:7). The fact that the baby was *her* firstborn Son rather than *their* first child attests to the fact that Mary's baby was not, in fact, Joseph's child. Gabriel's annunciation to Mary had made it clear that the promised child would, in fact, be "the Son of God" (Luke 1:35), which makes the humble circumstances of Jesus' birth all the more striking. That this child, who was to be not just the King of Israel but indeed the King of Heaven, was born in a setting so different from the palaces of Augustus or Herod is striking. Nevertheless, while this contrast is real and important, Luke's account of the couple's arrival in Bethlehem and Jesus' subsequent birth is nonetheless somewhat less clear on the details than tradition often assumes.

The traditional picture of the scene imagines the

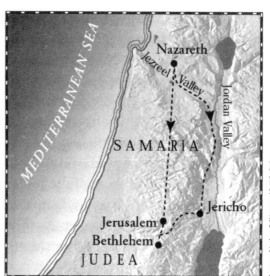

Courtesy of Andrew C. Skinner and D. Kelly Ogden.

Joseph and Mary could have taken one of two routes to Bethlehem. The direct route led through difficult terrain and through the territory of the potentially unfriendly Samaritans. The longer route through the Jezreel and Jordan Valleys was, in fact, easier.

Courtesy of Chad Emmett.

A view of modern Bethlehem in 1982.

couple arriving in a strange town, where they cannot find room in an inn. First, the word translated as *room* is *topos* in Greek, which simply means a place or space rather than an actual room in a commercial or private establishment. Taking Luke's notice of the census at face value, most readers assume that the reason there was no space for Joseph and Mary is that Bethlehem was overflowing with other people coming to enroll in their ancestral town. Second, the Greek term *katalyma,* rendered as *inn* in the King James Version, has a fairly broad range of meanings. Technically a *katalyma* was a place for setting down or laying down a burden. Derived from this basic definition are the possibilities that Luke meant a traditional inn or lodging; a camp on the road or a more permanent caravansary outside the town; or simply a guest room in some other type of building in Bethlehem itself.[14]

Conventionally the *katalyma* has been interpreted as a commercial travelers inn, where customers would pay for their lodging for the night. This interpretation led to the long-established image of a gruff innkeeper turning the couple away because he had no vacancies, shouting "No room!" though Luke does not suggest any such details. Further, when Luke does refer to this type of inn in the later story of the Good Samaritan, which does feature an innkeeper (Luke 10:34–35), he uses a different word for *inn,* the Greek word *pandocheion.* More in harmony with the period and culture, others suppose what Luke is referring to is a caravansary or *khan,* a rectangular walled area where traveling companies could lodge, keeping their animals in the central, uncovered area while most people stayed in niches or stalls along the exterior. Another possibility, however, is that *katalyma* here simply means "guest room," which is how Luke uses the same term in Luke 22:11, the only other time that he uses the word in his Gospel. In that passage it refers to the guest room that Jesus and his disciples use for

The Year of Jesus' Birth

Though settling on the date of Christmas as December 25 was a postbiblical development (see Introduction), attempts to identify the year of Jesus' birth have been based on several passages in the Infancy Narratives themselves. Matthew 2:1 and Luke 1:5 seem to place the birth before the death of Herod the Great in 4 B.C., a date which is also supported by Luke 3:1–2. On the other hand, Luke 2:2 dates the birth of Jesus to the governorship of Cyrenius, or Quirinius, which began in A.D. 6. This difference of at least ten years between these two dates cannot be reconciled easily with the evidence currently available.

Of course, neither of these dates accords with the modern Western calendar, which suggests that Jesus was born in A.D. 1, with A.D. standing for *anno Domini*, or "the year of our Lord." This dating system was established about A.D. 500 by a monk named Dionysius Exiguus, who calculated that Jesus was born 754 years after the traditional date of Rome's founding. With that point of reference, he reorganized the calendar, using Christ's birth as the central point—all events before his birth counting down to it and all after counting up from it. But because it is most likely that Christ's birth occurred on a date before Herod's death in 4 B.C., it is clear that Dionysius miscalculated.[15]

Given the probability that Jesus was born in 5 or 4 B.C., it is also probable that the notice in D&C 20:1 that the Church was reorganized "one thousand eight hundred and thirty years since the coming of our Lord and Savior Jesus Christ in the flesh" is a conventional date expression based on the calendar that Joseph Smith was using at the time.[16] Likewise, attempts to correlate Book of Mormon references to the birth and death of Jesus must take into account the complexities involved in correlating ancient calendars, including the differences between lunar and solar calendars (see Omni 1:21) and uncertainties about how or whether the Nephites practiced intercalation—adding days or other periods to the calendar to keep the calendar year in line with the seasons.[17]

the Last Supper. There we learn it is a furnished upper room apparently rented out at Passover time for just that purpose. In the case of the Nativity story, the guest room could have been any guest room in a commercial or private building that could be rented, probably to numerous guests, as temporary or long-term lodging.[18]

Given that Joseph may well have had family in Bethlehem, the guest room might have been in the home of a relative or even in his own family home. In the latter case, Joseph, who may have gone to Nazareth to retrieve his new bride and bring her home to Bethlehem, may have returned home to find that there was not sufficient room—or at least not any private space—for the new couple in what would have been a typical one- or two-room house.[19] There not being room for a woman in labor in

St. Joseph Seeks Lodging in Bethlehem, *by James Tissot.*

Wikimedia

the home of her new in-laws creates a scenario more poignant and more distressing than one of being turned away by strangers.

While many useful lessons can be drawn from any of the scenarios above, particularly the importance of our making room in our own hearts for the Savior, in reality none of these possibilities needs to reflect heartlessness on the part of others. Whether an inn, a caravansary, or a guest room, a *katalyma* would most likely have been shared with many other people and thus would not have afforded Joseph and Mary any seclusion during her labor. In that case, it may have been the couple's own decision to leave the crowded public area for the relative privacy of bedding in an area set aside for animals. The Joseph Smith Translation changes *inn* to *inns,* indicating that guest rooms in other homes—or perhaps all the stalls in a caravansary—were filled and there was nowhere else to go.[20]

Because of the reference to Mary placing her new baby in a manger, that area is often assumed to have been a stable, but it could have been the large central open space in a caravansary or perhaps even rudimentary pens in or near a private home. Since the second century, a certain cave in Bethlehem of the type that was sometimes used to stable animals has been identified as the place where Jesus was born,[21] though Luke gives no indication of this. Likewise, Luke does not give any other details, such as who might have attended during Mary's labor and delivery, though one can imagine an innkeeper's wife, fellow female travelers, or new in-laws. None of these particulars—or our lack of certainty about them—need detract, however, from the contrast that Luke creates between the circumstances of the birth of the baby Jesus and conditions that would have surrounded the birth of a king's or an emperor's son.

Luke carefully records that Mary wrapped the baby Jesus in swaddling clothes (Greek, *esparaganōsen*) and laid him in a manger, details that are important enough to be used in the angelic annunciation to the shepherds as signs to help them identify the promised baby (Luke 2:12). Wrapping a child in swaddling clothes in and of itself was not particularly unusual for the period, though certainly the simple linen strips with which Mary's baby was bound would contrast with the rich cloth

Making Room for Jesus

While the *katalyma* or inn where there was no room for Mary to give birth to Jesus might have been some type of commercial lodging, it is more likely that it was either a semi-private cubicle on the edge of a caravansary or the guest room in a private home. Likewise, there being no room "for them," may suggest that their humble state or lack of connections were what kept them from obtaining scarce space that night; if they had had money or had known the right people, perhaps room would have been made for them.[22]

Nevertheless, there being "no room" does not necessarily reflect heartlessness on the part of others. Whether a room in an inn, a caravansary cubicle, or a guest chamber, a *katalyma* would necessarily still have been shared with many other people and thus not have afforded Joseph and Mary with any seclusion during her labor.[23] Still, a valuable lesson can be drawn from there having been "no room for them in the inn." While others may not have made room for Jesus at his birth, Joseph and Mary did all that they could to provide a quiet, safe, and welcoming place for Jesus.

In today's world where many feel they have no need for Jesus, we must examine ourselves, asking whether we truly have made room for our Savior in our own hearts. What are we willing to do or sacrifice so that Christ can be born anew in our lives, filling us with the image of his countenance, changing our hearts, and making us more like him? (see Alma 5:14).

and ornamentation accompanying a royal or imperial birth. But the very fact that Jesus needed to be swaddled marks the humble state into which the divine Jehovah had condescended. Swaddling consisted of wrapping a baby tightly in strips of cloth, not just to serve as a rudimentary diaper but

also to keep the baby warm and its limbs straight. The practice was seen anciently as a sign of parental care, and that Jesus required such care is an indication that he had indeed "emptied himself," or set aside his premortal knowledge, power, and glory (see Philippians 2:7, where the Greek, *ekenōsen,* for "emptied himself" is translated in the KJV, "made himself of no reputation"; see also 1 Nephi 11:18–20; D&C 93:11–14). Ancient and modern commentators have sought additional

The Nativity, *etching by Carl Bloch.*

Courtesy of Kent Jackson.

Left: In the Church of the Nativity, an ornamental star marks the traditional birth spot of Jesus. Right: This carved stone manger, or feeding trough, may be similar to the one in which Mary laid the baby Jesus.

"Away in a Manger"

One of the most beloved Christmas carols is "Away in a Manger." Long incorrectly attributed to Martin Luther, the text of its first two verses was published anonymously in American Lutheran circles in 1885. In 1887, James R. Murray set the words to what has become the more standard American tune. The third verse was then published anonymously sometime before 1892. The tune more commonly sung in England was published by William James Kirkpatrick in 1895. This sweet carol, popular with children, treats the simple fact of Jesus' birth as recorded in Luke 2:7.[24]

Away in a manger, no crib for a bed,
The little Lord Jesus laid down His sweet head.
The stars in the sky looked down where he lay,
The little Lord Jesus asleep in the hay.

The cattle are lowing, the baby awakes,
But little Lord Jesus no crying he makes.
I love Thee, Lord Jesus, look down from the sky
And stay by my cradle til morning is nigh.

Be near me, Lord Jesus, I ask Thee to stay
Close by me forever, and love me, I pray.
Bless all the dear children in thy tender care,
And take us to heaven, to live with Thee there.[25]

symbolism in the sign of the swaddling clothes. As a parent swaddles and nurtures his or her child, so will this Christ child warm, protect, and offer security to us. Likewise, a parallel can be drawn between his swaddling clothes and the grave clothes that Jesus left in the empty tomb; his birth, perhaps in a cave, thus foreshadowing his burial in the garden tomb.[26]

The symbolism of carefully swaddling a baby seems incongruent with Mary's next act of placing the baby in a manger. This was, of course, a utilitarian act, keeping the baby off the ground and away from dirt and animal waste. The Greek word here translated as *manger* is *phatnē,* which refers to a crib, a wooden or stone feeding box or trough (the English word comes from the French *manger,* meaning "to eat"). Though a manger presupposes the presence of animals, Luke does not mention any and certainly does not specify oxen, donkeys, lambs, or any of the other "friendly beasts" often associated with the Nativity scene. Nevertheless, the attendance of animals upon the arrival of the newborn babe was suggested very early, perhaps as early Christians recognized that the word that Luke used, *phatnē,* also appears in the Septuagint version of Isaiah 1:3: "The ox knoweth his owner, and the ass his master's *crib:* but Israel doth not know, my people doth not consider" (emphasis added). This cross-reference and the symbolism it carries emphasizes that Jehovah's creatures knew and accepted him, whereas his people, both then and since, have not always done the same.

THE ANNUNCIATION TO THE SHEPHERDS

After Jesus is born and Mary places him in the manger, Luke changes scenes, taking the reader outside Bethlehem to the countryside where shepherds are watching their flocks (Luke 2:8). Because they and their animals were outside at night, it is unlikely that the event occurred during the winter. Rather, it is probable that it occurred in the spring, when sheep are lambing and require almost constant attention.[27] Exactly where the shepherds were that night is unknown, but in the late fourth century a woman named Egeria traveled from Gaul (now modern France) to the Holy Land on a pilgrimage. She reported in a letter home that there was a church outside Bethlehem called "at the shepherds," which a later traveler located about a mile east of the town. In that vicinity there are now two sites identified as "Shepherds' Fields." One, Kenisat

The largely Arab Christian village of Beit Sahour, just east of Bethlehem, lies near the spot where tradition holds that the angels appeared to the shepherds. The Roman Catholic church of Khirbet Siyar el-Ghanem commemorates this joyous event.

Courtesy of Chad Emmett.

Titles of the Messiah from Isaiah 9:6

That the Babe of Bethlehem was far more than a simple baby is made clear by the messianic titles ascribed to him in the prophetic description of Isaiah 9:6. Some scholars have tried to find this passage's original fulfillment in Hezekiah, who went on to be one of Judah's few righteous kings and hence, in some ways, a type of the coming Messiah (see Chapter 1: Son of David). Nevertheless, Isaiah's prophecy does not fit Hezekiah in all of its details; its ultimate fulfillment is found clearly in Jesus Christ. After proclaiming, "For unto us a child is born, unto us a son is given: and the government shall be upon his shoulder," Isaiah lists four titles, each consisting of a noun and its modifier:

> Wonderful Counsellor
> The mighty God
> The everlasting Father
> The Prince of Peace

A punctuation error in early English translations divided "Wonderful Counselor" into two different titles, separating them with a comma that disrupts the Hebrew construction. This mistake has been perpetuated most famously in the well-known *Messiah* chorus, "For unto Us a Child Is Born," in which Handel accentuated the incorrect punctuation by placing dramatic rests between the words "Wonderful" and "Counselor."

er-Ruwat, is owned by the Greek Orthodox Church and the other, Khirbet Siyar el-Ghanem, by the Roman Catholic Church.[28] In one of these locations, or nearby, shepherds were outside when an angel appeared to them, announcing the birth of the Promised Savior.

It is clearly significant that the announcement came first to shepherds. Though Matthew relates that the news is conveyed later to the Wise Men—no doubt representing the privileged and educated—via the means of astronomical phenomenon, the lowly shepherds in Luke were informed by direct revelation immediately after Jesus' birth.[29] There is a tendency to romanticize the shepherds, making them in our imagination good, gentle, humble figures. In actuality, shepherds at the time were often looked upon as unclean and outside the law, sometimes even as dishonest, because they often grazed their flocks on other people's lands. In this case, they fit well with Luke's emphasis elsewhere in his Gospel, where Jesus declares he has come not to the righteous but to the outcasts and sinners.[30] Others have noted, however, that many of the flocks near Bethlehem, which is only six miles from Jerusalem, were intended for temple sacrifices, in which case one sees an entirely different symbolism. Jesus came as the Lamb of God, to die for the sins of the world, and it was perhaps to the keepers of temple flocks that his birth was first announced. A particular site, Migdal Eder, or "the Tower of the Flock," is noted in connection with these sacred flocks. Mentioned in Genesis 35:21, it is also

A Palestinian shepherd leads his sheep among the hills around Bethlehem.

mentioned in Micah 4:8 as part of a larger oracle which includes the prophecy in Micah 5:2 that the Messiah will come from Bethlehem (see Chapter 4: King of Israel).[31]

Luke describes the angel who appeared to the shepherds as simply being "the angel of the Lord" (Luke 2:9). Matthew also uses this title when he describes Joseph's first visionary dream (Matthew 1:20). In both cases there is an echo of a common divine messenger who represents the Lord so powerfully and directly that he, or his words, are often interchanged with God himself. The sense then is that the message the angel delivers is directly from God, which is reinforced by Luke's description that "the glory of the Lord shone round about them."[32] As in the Old Testament, glory is a visible manifestation of God's power and radiance, sometimes even representing his presence. In view of this, the shepherds are understandably afraid, which proves to be the first step in the commissioning or annunciation pattern we have already seen with Zacharias and Mary (see Chapter 2: Promised Savior).

In the second step of this pattern, the messenger tells the frightened recipient—in this case recipients—not to be afraid. The announcement that follows is one of the most well-known passages in the Christmas story, one that summarizes the joy and gladness of this sacred event: "Fear not: for, behold, *I bring you good tidings of great joy,* which shall be to all people" (Luke 2:10; emphasis added). The single Greek verb *euangelizomai* yields the entire phrase "I bring you good tidings," and it shares the same stem as *euangellion,* meaning "good news" or "the gospel." While the birth of the True King was

Courtesy of Chad Emmett.

An open spot north of Bethlehem is an area frequently commemorated as "The Shepherds' Field" by many Latter-day Saint visitors.

certainly good news, the good tidings that would bring joy to all people is ultimately found in what Jesus would later do—suffer, die, and rise again—making the good news that of salvation.

In line with this, the angel of the Lord continues, "For unto you is born this day . . . a Saviour, which is Christ the Lord" (Luke 2:11). While the idea that God is a savior who rescues his people is certainly present in Hebrew prophecy, the Greek word for "savior" (*sōtēr*) had particular political implications in the context of a Roman-governed state, suggesting the political or temporal benefits that a worldly ruler provided his subjects. This is the same context in which Luke places the Nativity by beginning it with a reference to Augustus. For Luke, however, the source of salvation, peace, and prosperity is not the Roman emperor but the Anointed One promised by God. Then, by equating this Christ with "the Lord," Luke further identifies the baby as the divine Jehovah, since the Greek *kyrios* and Hebrew *adonai* ("lord") were both substitutes for the divine name YHWH.[33]

Despite the majestic identity of the baby, the angel gives the shepherds what seems like

Courtesy of Chad Emmett.

In 1982, Elder Howard W. Hunter (seated) addressed a group of Latter-day Saints on Christmas Eve.

"Angels, from the Realms of Glory"

In 1816, James Montgomery (1771–1854) published a new carol that connected the angels' song at the first Christmas to the primeval shout of the morning stars at the foundation of the earth (Job 38:4–7):

> Angels, from the realms of glory,
> Wing your flight o'er all the earth;
> Ye who sang Creation's story
> Now proclaim Messiah's birth.

Like many carols, it brings together both Infancy Narratives, addressing the shepherds of Luke 2 in the second verse before moving to the sages—that is, the Wise Men—of Matthew 2 in the third verse. The fourth and fifth verses tie the events of the Nativity to the glorious return and millennial reign of Jesus, addressing it to Saints of all ages:

> Saints, before the altar bending.   Though an infant now we view him,
> Watching long in hope and fear: He shall fill his Father's throne,
> Suddenly the Lord, descending,   Gather all the nations to him;
> In his temple shall appear.   Every knee shall then bow down.[34]

Although it was later also sung in English to a tune by Henry Smart (1813–1867) known as "Regent Square," Montgomery's song was originally sung to an eighteenth-century French carol called *Les Anges dans Nos Campagnes*.[35] This French melody, also the tune used for "Angels, We Have Heard on High," has become familiar to LDS audiences because of the popular Mack Wilberg arrangement sung by the Mormon Tabernacle Choir at the conclusion of its annual Christmas concert.

Originally, "Angels, from the Realms of Glory" ended with the repeated refrain, "Come and worship Christ the newborn King!" but now frequently uses the same ending as "Angels, We Have Heard on High," repeating in Latin the words of the angels that first Christmas night: "Gloria in Excelsis Deo!"

an incongruous sign: "And this shall be a sign unto you; Ye shall find the babe wrapped in swaddling clothes, lying in a manger" (Luke 2:12). The swaddling in itself was not likely to be the sign that the shepherds would recognize, because swaddling was a sign of parental concern and care for a newborn. Rather, finding a newborn child in a feeding trough would be the sign unusual enough that the shepherds would know they had found the correct baby.

Yet before the shepherds can hurry to Bethlehem to find a child swaddled in a manger, the angel who had been speaking to them is joined by an angelic choir praising God—much as they had when they "shouted for joy" at the creation (Job 38:7). Their song constitutes the briefest—but no doubt

The Annunciation to the Shepherds, *by Abraham Hondius.*

Each year, the Christmas concert of the Mormon Tabernacle Choir ends with Mack Wilberg's arrangement of "Angels, from the Realms of Glory." A magnificent finale involving the Choir, the Orchestra at Temple Square, the Bells at Temple Square, guest artists, and dancers, the rendition follows a reading of Luke 2:1–14. This production number seeks to recreate the joy that accompanied the angel's announcement of Christ's birth. During its reprise, the audience of more than 21,000 is invited to join the performers in giving glory to God with a final chorus of "Gloria Deo!"

best-known (perhaps because it is the briefest)—of the four canticles in Luke's Infancy Narrative. Known as the *Gloria in Excelsis* from its traditional title in Latin, it has entered the liturgy of several churches as well as the music of countless songs. While textual evidence suggests several possible renderings of the song (see "Peace on Earth—to Whom?" page 83), the version well-known from the King James Version of the Bible is: "Glory to God in the highest, and on earth peace, good will toward men" (Luke 2:14). The lack of a verb in each phrase of the song suggests a Semitic original that Luke or his source translated into Greek. In addition to being a simple declaration, it is possible that the missing verb "to be" is intended to be imperative or jussive (commanding) in force, meaning that it is a prayer that glory *be* to God and peace *be* on earth.

The expression "in the highest" in English can be taken to be an expression of degree, suggesting that the angels were giving God the highest praise, but in Greek the prepositional phrase *en hypsistois* is more likely to be locational, describing where the glory should be found. *Hypsistois* can be either masculine or neuter plural, so there is the possibility that the glory is to be found "among the highest ones," perhaps meaning among angels or other divine beings, though the most likely meaning is that the glory should be in the highest places, meaning in the heavens. This finds an important echo later in Luke's account of Christ's Triumphal Entry, when those who welcome Jesus as he approaches Jerusalem prior to his Passion cry out, "Blessed be the King that cometh in the name of the Lord:

Peace on Earth—to Whom?

Although "Glory to God in the highest, and on earth peace, good will toward men" has become one of the best-known Christmas wishes, the difference of a single letter in some Greek manuscripts produces different possible meanings of this familiar expression from Luke 2:14. Many later Greek manuscripts read *eudokia* for "good will," making it a nominative form, parallel to the nouns for "glory" and "peace." The following direct translation of the traditional rendering reflects the Greek word order and produces a canticle of three fairly parallel phrases:

> *Glory in the highest to God*
> *And on earth peace*
> *Among men good will*

These three phrases convey a directional or locational pattern: glory *to* God, peace *on* earth, and good will *to* men. These Greek manuscripts formed the basis of the printed Greek editions of the New Testament used by both the King James translators of the English Bible and by Martin Luther for his German translation.

Some surviving early manuscripts, however, read *eudokias* instead of *eudokia*.[36] This difference of a single letter makes the noun a genitive rather than a nominative. This genitive form can then have two different grammatical functions, either a genitive of description or an objective genitive. This produces two different possible translations, each consisting of just two phrases instead of three:

> *Glory in the highest to God*   *Glory in the highest to God*
> *And on earth peace to men of good will*   *And on earth peace to men whom [God] favors*

When Jerome translated the Bible into Latin in the fourth century, he used an earlier manuscript and followed the meaning "peace to men of good will." As a result, this is the version of the canticle common to most Catholic Bibles. Because most modern English translations also favor earlier manuscripts, the two readings of the genitive *eudokias* have become increasingly more common.

Anecdotal evidence suggests that during World War I, when these new translations were first beginning to circulate, wartime feelings at times influenced which version people accepted. The implication of the descriptive genitive, "peace to men of good will," was that, in that conflict, peace ought to be the property of men of good will, as opposed to those seen as aggressors. Today, the objective genitive interpretation, "whom God favors," is becoming progressively more frequent in both scholarly and some Protestant circles.[37]

While "peace, good will to men," "peace to men of good will," and "peace to those whom God favors" all have significantly different meanings, they each represent an important theological truth. God does, in fact, desire peace on earth and has good will toward all men and women. But it is also true that lasting peace will not exist on earth unless people themselves have good will, first toward one another, and, more importantly, toward God—accepting the gift of his Son and letting his peace come into their lives.[38] Finally, while God loves all his children, he blesses and hence favors those whom he chooses because of their faith and obedience.

Adoration of the Shepherds, *by Bartolomé Esteban Murillo.*

peace in heaven, and *glory in the highest*" (Luke 19:38; emphasis added). Thus the hosts of heaven at Jesus' birth and the multitude on earth before his Passion form antiphonal choruses bracketing Christ's mission, the angels praying for peace on earth and the crowds praying for peace in heaven.[39]

Yet both groups ascribe all glory to God in the highest heavens, even as the premortal Christ himself pledged all glory from his mission to God his Father (Moses 4:2). The result of Jesus' saving mission would be peace on the earth—peace in individual hearts, within families and friendships, and between groups and nations. But ultimately the mission of this precious baby would be to reestablish peace between God and his children, reconciling us through the atoning death of his Only Begotten Son and bringing us true joy (see Romans 5:8–11).

THE ADORATION OF THE SHEPHERDS

Luke reports that as soon as the angels departed, the shepherds encouraged each other to go to Bethlehem to find the promised child. Significantly, they did not go to see *whether* the saying of the angel was true but rather simply to "see this thing *which is come to pass,* which the Lord hath made known unto us" (Luke 2:15; emphasis added). Unlike Zacharias, who seems to have been uncertain whether the miracle promised to him would happen, the shepherds simply accept their angelic direction and "came with haste, and found Mary, and Joseph, and the babe lying in a manger" (Luke 2:16). Luke provides no detail as to how the shepherds found the family; unlike the Wise Men later described by Matthew, they do not seem to have had a star to guide them. Though they may have had other ways of finding the baby Jesus, the only indication that Luke gives was that finding a child in the unexpected cradle of a manger was their sign, because finding a swaddled child would not have been in itself unusual.

Verse 16 is Luke's third mention of a manger, or *phatnē.* Shepherds coming to the manger more closely ties Luke's usage of that word to the same word in the Septuagint rendering of Isaiah 1:3. We have suggested that later Christian imaginings of this scene perhaps included oxen and donkeys because of Isaiah's mention of "his master's crib" (*phatnē*), but as we have seen Luke does not mention any animals. He does mention, however, that *shepherds* came to the manger. So while Israel in Isaiah's day did not know or recognize the Lord, these few representatives of Israel at the first Christmas believed the angel's word, followed his command to go to Bethlehem, and indeed found their Master swaddled there.[40] They, then, were the oxen who knew their owner and the donkeys who came to their master's crib.

In art the scene that follows is traditionally known as "the Adoration of the Shepherds," but Luke does not record what the shepherds did when they arrived, although one can imagine that they would have gazed at the child in wonder, probably paying reverent homage (Greek, *prosekynēsan;* KJV, "worshipped"), as Matthew records that the Wise Men did (Matthew 2:11). Instead, Luke simply says that "when they had seen it, they *made known abroad* the saying which was told them concerning this child" (Luke 2:17; emphasis added). The term that Luke uses for "made known abroad" is *egnōrisan,* which conveys the idea not only of "making known" but also "pointing out" and "explaining."[41] In a sense, they were the forerunners of the later Apostles, who were the shepherds whom Christ would call to lead his Church.

All who hear their report are astonished (Greek, *ethaumasan;* Luke 2:18), just as those who were present when Zacharias began to speak again at the circumcision and naming of John had marveled (also *ethaumasan;* Luke 1:63). When the tidings of John the Baptist were spread throughout the hill country of Judea, all who heard it "laid them up in their hearts" and wondered what kind of child he would be. Yet while the shepherds spread the news around Bethlehem, only Mary "kept all these things, and pondered them in her heart" (Luke 2:19). By the time Jesus' public ministry began, there was little common knowledge or public memory of the great night of Jesus' birth, leading Raymond Brown to observe that while Mary heard and treasured the shepherds' testimony, many others with whom the shepherds shared their witness were like those in the Parable of the Sower who, though receiving the word with joy, had no roots of their own in their faith and fell away (see Luke 8:13).[42]

Courtesy of Kent Jackson.

Like the shepherds that first Christmas, modern pilgrims flock around the traditional site of Jesus' birth to pay homage.

Mitt hjerte alltid vanker
"My Heart Doth Always Wander"

In 1732, a Danish bishop named Hans Adolph Brorson (1694–1764) wrote a poem about the birth of Jesus that brings the reader into the experience of the shepherds that first Christmas night. As they viewed the holy baby cradled in the manger, so should we cradle him in our hearts.[43] In the second to last verse, Brorson's lyrics also allude to Jesus' triumphal entry—at the end of his ministry and, perhaps, at his glorious return—with a mention of palm leaves, before concluding with a pledge that we should give our lives to the Savior and forever treasure him within our hearts.

My heart doth always wander	To my heart be no stranger—
To Jesus' manger bed.	Thy home it e'er shall be.
His lowly birth I ponder;	And as within the manger
To him my thoughts are led.	My love shall cradle thee.
My yearning finds assurance,	Thy holy crib I'll honor
And faith renews so bright,	And round it palm leaves lay.
When I recall with reverence	To Thee alone, dear Savior,
That blessed Christmas night.	I give my life each day.
Ah, come dear Lord be with me,	Come, grant me heav'nly pleasure
And in my heart reside.	And true delight impart.
Sweet comfort Thou shalt give me;	For Thou art my soul's treasure,
Come, Jesus, here abide.	Born deep within my heart.[44]

Set to a Norwegian folk tune, Brorson's poem has become a popular Christmas song in Scandinavia today, sung by such noted vocalists as Sissel Kyrkjebø. Its Norwegian title translates literally as "My Heart Doth Always Wander," but it is also known in English as "That Blessed Christmas Night."

Perhaps Mary recognized in the humble shepherds a fulfillment of a phrase in her own prophetic song, the *Magnificat,* when she said, "He hath put down the mighty from their seats, and exalted them of low degree" (Luke 1:52). Whereas the mighty, represented by King Herod and Emperor Augustus in the Infancy Narratives, dwelled in palaces and enjoyed all the good things of the world, in this most humble of settings these men, hungry for the things of God, were being spiritually "filled . . . with good things" (Luke 1:53), namely the good news of God's gift to them and to us.

The shepherds, having reported the angels' message to Joseph and Mary and having seen—and no doubt adored—the baby Jesus, "returned, glorifying and praising God for all the things that they had

Pondering in Her Heart: Mary and the Baby Jesus

Gabriel first planted in Mary's heart the seeds of the testimony of who her son would be, but afterward she may not have fully understood what all this would entail. Just as Jesus did not receive a "fulness at the first, but received grace for grace" (D&C 93:12), Mary's knowledge and conviction must have grown and deepened with time. The shepherds' report of further angelic affirmation no doubt strengthened her faith in Jesus' divine identity. Further confirmation would come from the witnesses of Simeon and Anna in the temple (see Luke 2:25–48), and indeed later from the boy Jesus himself (see Luke 2:49). Nevertheless, Mary's own knowledge of who Jesus was would continue to grow as she watched his life and ministry unfold, culminating in that terrible moment when she stood at the foot of his cross and beheld him die for the sins of the world (see John 19:25). Indeed, from his divine conception and miraculous birth to his atoning death, there was

In the Arms of Mary, by Simon Dewey.

no greater mortal witness of the Savior than his own mother.

Still, those events lay far beyond that first night, when Mary gazed at her baby lying in the manger. Despite what an angel had already told her—indeed, despite what she had already experienced when the power of the Highest had overshadowed her—she may well have wondered exactly how the angel's promises would come to pass and what her son's life would be like. On a different scale, this is the experience that any father or mother can have when gazing at his or her child. As Elaine Cannon has written, "Like Mary, they rear their babies into manhood equal to serving the Lord according to their own particular missions in life."[45]

I remember distinctly and warmly the feelings that my wife, Elaine, expressed the first Christmas Eve after Samuel was born. That night she understood Mary's story perhaps more than she ever had before. Our son is also special, as is every boy and girl born on this earth. In our case, our son has special needs, but special gifts as well.

heard and seen" (Luke 2:20). While their efforts in spreading the good news did not have the kind of lasting results that the ministry of the later Apostles would have, their experience that night no doubt made an indelible impression upon their souls, making them lifetime witnesses of Jesus' birth.[46] Like them, we too should rejoice in the events of that night, praising and thanking God for his great gift to us. As Alonzo Gaskill has written, "As followers of Christ—and bearers of the divine witness that He is the Messiah, the Savior, He who lives—we should follow the example of these foreordained shepherds and lift our voices regarding the greatest miracle of all time—for, like them, we too have marvelous things to declare."[47]

THE BABE IN THE TEMPLE

Luke continues his Infancy Narrative by telling of the circumcision of the baby eight days after his birth, when he was named in accordance with revelation. Jesus' circumcision and naming is directly parallel to John's circumcision and naming (see Luke 1:59–79), though here the ritual is recounted in a single verse (Luke 2:21).[48] Since Abraham—even before the law of Moses—circumcising a male child on the eighth day after his birth was an outward sign of belonging to the covenant (see Genesis 17:11–13; Acts 7:8). As was John, Jesus was born under the law (KJV, Galatians 4:4, "made under the law"), but while John's ministry was primarily for the benefit of Israel, Jesus' ministry would be to *all* peoples, perhaps accounting for Luke's briefer account here. At his circumcision, the child received the name *Jesus* in accordance with Gabriel's annunciation. Then Luke moves quickly to an episode for which John the Baptist's birth had no parallel yet was rich with symbolism of Jesus' mission. In this account, Luke's attention is centered on two prophetic figures, Simeon and the aged widow Anna (Hebrew, *Ḥannah*), making their stories the focus of the scene.

Jesus' parents take him to the temple—technically for Mary's purification forty days after childbirth and also as an opportunity to present Jesus to God, which gives this episode its traditional name, the Presentation. Leviticus 12:1–8 mandated that forty days after a woman gave birth, she had to be purified of ritual uncleanliness.[49] As diligent keepers of the law of Moses,

A beautiful olive wood crèche by George Lama of Bethlehem adorns the Brigham Young University Jerusalem Center at Christmastime.

Courtesy of Chad Emmett.

The Christmas Crèche

A common way of commemorating the scene of Jesus' birth is to set up a Nativity scene, also known as a *crèche* (Old French, meaning "manger" or "crib"). A crèche can be as simple as figures of Joseph, Mary, and the baby Jesus in a manger. Other figures such as shepherds are common additions, following Luke's narrative. Other common elements, such as the Wise Men and a star above the manger, come from later events described by Matthew in Matthew 2. The stable and various animals have no basis in the Infancy Narratives themselves, but are reasonable additions. The ox and donkey are derived from Isaiah 1:3, and the Wise Men's camels have antecedents in a prophecy found in Isaiah 60:6, connected to the Wise Men because of its reference to bringing gold and incense to honor the house of Israel.

Courtesy of Art Resource. Used by permission.

An early Christian fresco from the Catacomb of Priscilla in Rome, dating from the third or possibly second century A.D. depicts Mary and the Baby together with a prophet and a star.

The earliest portrayal of the Nativity in art may be funerary paintings in the Roman catacombs of St. Sebastian and Priscilla, dating as early as A.D. 380. The practice of setting up a three-dimensional representation of the Nativity scene began with St. Francis of Assisi, who staged a living nativity scene in Greccio, Italy, in 1223. St. Francis's effort, which used a peasant family and placed the baby in a hay-filled crib, was meant to refocus Christmas celebrations on the actual humble birth of the Savior.[50]

Although many homes set up a complete crèche early in the Christmas season, most churches that set up a crèche do not place the baby Jesus in the manger until Christmas Eve, and some do not introduce the Magi until January 6, the Feast of Epiphany, which in Western churches celebrates the arrival of the Wise Men.

Simeon and then Anna would have found Jesus somewhere in the courts of the Temple of Herod.

Joseph and Mary took advantage of their proximity to Jerusalem to make the appropriate offering at the temple in connection with her purification. Although the designated offering was a yearling lamb and a dove, they took advantage of the alternative that the Law allowed the poor, substituting a pair of doves. References to Mary's purification in Luke 2:22 and 24 frame references to a second ceremony, the redemption of the firstborn, in Luke 2:22–23. After the Lord delivered the children of Israel from Egypt, he claimed the firstborn of every family in return for sparing them on the first Passover, requiring them to be consecrated to his service (see Exodus 13:2, 12–15). Although the Lord later accepted the service of the entire tribe of Levi in place of the firstborn of all Israel, he still required that the firstborn be redeemed by the price of five shekels (Numbers 18:15–16).

The redemption of the firstborn did not need to take place in the temple, but the holy family's presence in the sanctuary for Mary's purification provided Luke with an opportunity for some important symbolism. While we can assume that Joseph and Mary paid the five shekels required by the law,[51] by not mentioning the actual payment Luke implies that Jesus *continued* in the service of God rather than being redeemed from it. In this, the story of the Old Testament prophet Samuel serves as an anticipation. After their son had been weaned, Elkanah and Hannah brought the boy Samuel to the sanctuary at Shiloh, where he was presented and left for a lifetime of service to God (1 Samuel 1:24–28).[52] Recalling how Hannah's song served as a model for Mary's own *Magnificat* strengthens the connection, suggesting that Mary too was willingly presenting her son to God. While Jesus does not remain in the temple after his presentation, during his later boyhood visit he makes clear that he belongs there and that his mission is to be about his Father's business (Luke 2:46–49; see Conclusion: Remembering Christmas).

In some Christian traditions, the Presentation in the Temple is commemorated with an annual feast on February 2, forty days after Christmas. When the Presentation is observed, it emphasizes Jesus' presence in the temple. In the Anglican tradition, it is called "Candlemas," recounting the sacred lights of the temple. In Eastern Orthodoxy, however, an alternative name for the Presentation

Simeon in the Temple, *by Rembrandt Harmensz van Rijn.*

is *Hypapante,* or the Meeting of the Lord.[53] That name reflects an important emphasis in Luke's account—the family's presence in the temple allowed them to meet Simeon and Anna, who had been spiritually prepared to serve as powerful witnesses of the baby and his mission.

The Hebrew name *Šimʿon* (Greek, *Symeōn,* hence Symeon or Simeon) may mean both "[YHWH] had heard" and "one who hears and obeys." While numerous early Christian legends were propagated about Simeon,[54] Luke simply introduces him by describing Simeon as "*just* and devout, waiting for the *consolation* of Israel: and the Holy Ghost was upon him" (Luke 2:25; emphasis added). Just as Zacharias, Elisabeth, and Joseph were described as being just, or in harmony with the law (Greek, *dikaios*), so Simeon is presented as a righteous Israelite. The term translated as *consolation* is the Greek *paraklēsin;* in addition to meaning help, comfort, or relief, in origin it means "summons" or "encouragement," and it has the same root as "Comforter" (*paraklētos;* see John 14:16, 26; 15:26; 16:7).[55] This Simeon at the beginning of Jesus' story finds a certain parallel with Joseph of Arimathaea at its end: that Joseph is also just, waits for the kingdom of God, and, in taking Jesus down from the cross and burying him, likewise takes him in his arms (see Luke 23:50–53).[56]

This good man, assumed to be elderly and approaching death because of his subsequent words, had received a promise through the Holy Ghost "that he should not see death, before he had seen the Lord's Christ" (Luke 2:26). Accordingly, the Spirit brought him to the temple at just the right time to encounter the holy family, whereupon he takes the child in his arms and blesses him (Luke 2:28).

At that moment, Simeon blesses God and utters an inspired song, the fourth and final canticle in Luke's Infancy Narrative (Luke 2:29–32). By tradition it is known as the *Nunc Demittis,* from the Latin for the first line: "*Now you are sending away* your servant in peace" (KJV, "Lord, now lettest thou thy servant depart in peace, according to thy word"). Having at last seen the promised Savior, Simeon feels that he can die comforted and reassured, "for mine eyes have seen thy salvation." He continues by describing this salvation in terms rich with Old Testament allusions (see Psalm 98:3; Isaiah 40:5; 42:6; 49:6; 52:9–10).[57] When Zacharias sings of salvation in the *Benedictus,* his prophecy centers on the deliverance that will come to Israel. Simeon, in contrast, speaks of how Christ has been prepared for *all* people, and he balances both the Gentiles and the house of Israel in the final line, calling Christ "a light to lighten the Gentiles, and the glory of thy people Israel" (Luke 2:32).

Concluding the canticle, Simeon turns to Mary and speaks a final prophecy, telling her, "this child is set for the fall and rising again of many in Israel; and for a sign which shall be spoken against" (Luke 2:34), prophesying that while Jesus was the glory of Israel, many of his own people would reject him and he would cause divisions even within families (see Luke 12:51–53). Finally, Simeon alludes to the Passion and death of Jesus that Mary would witness so poignantly, telling her that her own soul would be pierced, but that in the end, judgment would come through her son's sacrifice (Luke 2:35; John 19:25, 33–34).[58] Writing of Simeon's seemingly gloomy prophecy to Mary, Elder Jeffrey R. Holland has testified, "The true meaning, the unique and lasting and joyous meaning of the birth of this baby, would be in the life he would lead and espe-

The Presentation of Jesus in the Temple, by James Tissot.

cially in his death, in his triumphant atoning sacrifice . . . , and in his prison-bursting resurrection."[59]

Luke's narrative provides a second witness in the temple in the person of Anna, an elderly widow who spent every day in the temple in prayer and fasting (Luke 2:36–37). Significantly, she is described as a prophetess, connecting her to Deborah, Huldah, the wife of Isaiah, and perhaps Samuel's mother, Hannah.[60] Indeed, *Anna* is a Greek transliteration of the Hebrew name *Ḥannah,* providing yet another connection between the story of Jesus' birth and that of the prophet Samuel. At a time when most Jews were from the tribes of Judah, Benjamin, and Levi, Luke notes that Anna was from the tribe of Asher, perhaps suggesting that the lost tribes of Israel also await the coming of Christ. Having married young, perhaps between ten and fourteen, she had lost her husband after seven years, and, depending upon how the next verse is read, she was either eighty-four years old or had lived another eighty-four years after her husband's death, which would mean she was as old as 103 or 105.[61] While the actual words of this faithful woman are not preserved, as Simeon's had been, she first blesses or thanks God and then "spake [Greek, *elalei,* or "kept speaking"] of him to all them that looked for redemption in Jerusalem" (Luke 2:38).

Simeon and Believers Today

The image of the aged Simeon in the temple, at last meeting his promised Savior, is one that resonates with many believers today. It is also an image that has come to have special, personal meaning to me. In 2010, just four days before Christmas, my grandfather Cannon Huntsman died. Two days after Christmas, we buried him. Funerals at Christmastime are always poignant, even when they are held for good men and women who die at an old age. The sense of loss and sadness can weigh heavily on and even dampen the Christmas spirit.

But it was the story of Simeon that gave me great comfort the day after that Christmas. I read it that night to Elaine and the children, and I decided to use it in my remarks at the funeral the next day. As long as health permitted, Grandpa had spent as much time as he could in the temple. And like Simeon, he had a powerful faith in his Savior and Redeemer. While he did not hold the baby Jesus in his arms nor see the risen Lord in the flesh, Grandpa had seen the hand of the Lord all his life and rejoiced in his testimony of Jesus.

While modern revelation tells us "thou shalt live together in love insomuch that thou shalt weep for the loss of them that die," it also reassures us that "those that die in me shall not taste of death, for it shall be sweet unto them" (D&C 42:45, 46). I have come to believe that men and women of Christ, like Grandpa, can share the sentiment of Simeon when their time comes, crying out in their hearts, "Lord, now lettest thou thy servant depart in peace" (Luke 2:29).

THE CONCLUSION OF LUKE'S STORY

After Anna's testimony, Luke brings his Infancy Narrative to a formal close. Just as Elkanah and Hannah returned to their home after taking Samuel to the sanctuary at Shiloh, so Joseph and Mary, after presenting Jesus in the Jerusalem temple, "returned into Galilee, to their own city Nazareth" (Luke 2:39). By ending his account of the Savior's birth with the episode of Jesus' presentation in the temple, Luke reminds us of how the story began—with Zacharias standing and praying in that same sacred place. The temple thus frames all of Luke's narrative, reminding us how and where we too can meet the Lord and commit ourselves to bringing him into the world, accomplishing his purposes, and bearing testimony of him as did Zacharias and Elisabeth, Mary and Joseph, and Simeon and Anna.

After the family's return to Galilee, in a parallel to the close of John the Baptist's story in Luke 1:80, Luke reports, "And the child grew, and waxed strong in spirit, filled with wisdom: and the grace of God was upon him" (Luke 2:40). The Babe of Bethlehem would return once more to the temple as a boy, but for the rest of Luke's Gospel he is Jesus of Nazareth, encouraging us to not end our celebration of Jesus Christ with the stories of his birth, but to move on with the marvelous accounts of his life, death, and Resurrection. ❖

THE ADVENT THEME OF JOY

Luke's account of the Savior's birth, complete with the angel's annunciation of "good tidings of great joy," provides one of the most joyful scenes in scripture. Traditionally the third Sunday of Advent is known
as *Gaudete Sunday,* from the Latin injunction "Rejoice!" Frequently read
on this Sunday is the verse, "Rejoice in the Lord alway: and again I say,
Rejoice" (Philippians 4:4). While the entire season leading up to Christmas
is a joyful period today, historically Advent was largely a solemn season of preparation. Gaudete Sunday was a welcome reminder that the
Christmas message is, in fact, one of happiness and rejoicing.

As a result, the third candle in many Advent wreaths is often pink or
rose-colored, setting it off from the other three purple candles. I find another useful image in the pink candle, choosing to see it as representing
the blood of Christ that he shed in his Passion, reminding us in the midst
of Christmas preparations that Jesus came into the world foremost as a
sacrifice. Nevertheless, the sorrow of Christ's suffering and death is blot-
ted out as we triumph in his Resurrection, and we anticipate the return of
Jesus in his Second Coming with joy.

Courtesy of Eric Huntsman.

*Advent wreath with three candles lit. The
pink candle, along with the earlier two
purple candles, is lit on the third Sunday of
Advent to celebrate the joy of Jesus' birth
and promised return.*

Many scriptures describe the joy that comes because of Christ's coming
and the salvation that he accomplished for us. The following are some of our
family's favorites, which we read together on the third Sunday of Advent:

"Behold, God is my salvation; I will trust, and not be afraid: for the Lord JEHOVAH is my strength and my song; he also
is become my salvation. *Therefore with joy shall ye draw water out of the wells of salvation*" (Isaiah 12:2–5; emphasis added).

"And he said unto me: Awake, and hear the words which I shall tell thee; for behold, I am come *to declare unto you
the glad tidings of great joy.* For the Lord hath heard thy prayers, and hath judged of thy righteousness, and hath sent
me to declare unto thee that thou mayest rejoice; and that thou mayest declare unto thy people, *that they may also be
filled with joy*" (Mosiah 3:3–4; emphasis added; see Chapter 5: Further Glad Tidings).

"Verily, verily, I say unto you, That ye shall weep and lament, but the world shall rejoice: and ye shall be sorrowful,
but your sorrow shall be turned into joy. A woman when she is in travail hath sorrow, because her hour is come: but as
soon as she is delivered of the child, she remembereth no more the anguish, for joy that a man is born into the world.
And ye now therefore have sorrow: but I will see you again, and your heart shall rejoice, and *your joy no man taketh
from you*" (John 16:20–22; emphasis added).

If the candles of the Advent wreath are also used to recall or teach about the covenants that God has made with us,
the third candle can be used to represent the covenant that God made with Israel through Moses. On one level, it represents the law of Moses, so the pink color of this candle can be used to remember the blood of that law's offerings, which
prefigured the sacrifice of Jesus Christ.

The best-known carol that sings of joy is, of course, "Joy to the World." The text is a Christian paraphrase of Psalm 98 by

Isaac Watts (1674–1748), and it was firmly associated with the hymn tune "Antioch" by Lowell Mason (1792–1872) in 1836.[1] Popular with Christian groups, many churches have adjusted the lyrics slightly to accord with their own beliefs or sensitivities.[2] Latter-day Saints are no different, following W. W. Phelps's lead by changing "and heaven and nature sing" in the last three lines of the first verse to "and saints and angels sing."[3] Because it is both familiar and fun to sing, our family always sings this carol at the end of our third Advent celebration.

Samuel with our Advent wreath and Christmas tree after lighting the third candle.

While "Joy to the World" may be a natural and easy Christmas carol to sing in connection with this Advent theme, I am personally attracted to "Jesu, Joy of Man's Desiring," though it is not strictly a Christmas song. From Bach's cantata *Herz und Mund und Tat und Leben*, the English rendition most commonly sung certainly catches the joy and mystery found in the incarnation of the Son of God as Jesus Christ:

Jesu, joy of man's desiring,
Holy wisdom, love most bright;
Drawn by Thee, our souls aspiring
Soar to uncreated light.

Word of God, our flesh that fashioned,
With the fire of life impassioned,
Striving still to truth unknown,
Soaring, dying round Thy throne.[4]

Because I like to link the third candle's pink color to both the Advent theme of joy and to the anticipation of Jesus' saving blood, I also like to read through or think about the words of the carol "The Holly and the Ivy." This traditional English carol was set to a French melody by Cecil Sharp (1859–1924) in 1911. Employing pre-Christian symbols, it nonetheless powerfully anticipates the Passion of Christ:

The holly and the ivy,
When they are both full grown,
Of all the trees that are in the wood,
The holly bears the crown.

The holly bears a blossom
As white as lily flower,
And Mary bore sweet Jesus Christ
To be our sweet Savior.

The holly bears a berry
As red as any blood;

And Mary bore sweet Jesus Christ
To do poor sinners good.

The holly bears a prickle
As sharp as any thorn;
And Mary bore sweet Jesus Christ
On Christmas Day in the morn.

The holly bears a bark
As bitter as any gall;
And Mary bore sweet Jesus Christ
For to redeem us all.[5]

4
KING OF ISRAEL

Matthew 2

*Now when Jesus was born in Bethlehem of Judea in the days of Herod the king,
behold, there came wise men from the east to Jerusalem, saying, Where is he that is born King
of the Jews? for we have seen his star in the east, and are come to worship him.*

—Matthew 2:1–2

Matthew's earlier, rather concise notice of Jesus' birth (Matthew 1:25; see Chapter 1: Son of David) is followed in his narrative by a carefully crafted series of episodes that depict the newborn King in the context of worldly rulers—notably Herod the Great, but also one of his sons and, by comparison, Pharaoh of Egypt. Whereas Matthew 1 demonstrates who Jesus was through an account of Jesus' genealogy and his divine conception, Matthew 2 emphasizes aspects of his messianic mission by focusing on the places where Jesus was born and lived. Woven into this narrative is the story of the Magi (or Wise Men), who come seeking the true King of the Jews. Their visit begins a series of events that result in the holy family's flight from Bethlehem to Egypt and their eventual relocation to Nazareth, where Jesus lives until he begins his public ministry. Through the use of his characteristic formula quotations, Matthew shows that many of these events are, in fact, the fulfillment of prophecy.

Many elements of this section of Matthew's Infancy Narrative have become, through depictions in art and music, familiar parts of our Christmas story. At times, however, harmonizing them with Luke's account keeps us from seeing some of the unique details and symbolism that Matthew carefully worked out. As in Matthew 1, Joseph continues to be a central figure, following the pattern

> ### Episodes of Matthew 2
>
> - The Story of the Wise Men (Epiphany, Matthew 2:1–12)
>   - Prophecy fulfilled: "Out of thee shall come a Governor" (Matthew 2:6 = Micah 5:2, 2 Samuel 5:2)
> - The Escape into Egypt (Matthew 2:13–15)
>   - Prophecy fulfilled: "Out of Egypt have I called my son" (Matthew 2:15 = Hosea 11:1)
> - The Massacre of the Innocents (Matthew 2:16–18)
>   - Prophecy fulfilled: "Rachel weeping for her children" (Matthew 2:18 = Jeremiah 31:15)
> - Return to Nazareth (Matthew 2:19–23)
>   - "He shall be called a Nazarene" (Matthew 2:23 = perhaps Judges 13:2–7; 1 Samuel 1:11, 22; Isaiah 11:1)
> - Conclusion of Matthew's Story (Matthew 2:23; JST, Matthew 3:24)

Adoration of the Magi, by Jean-Baptiste Jouvenet. Courtesy Bridgeman Art Library.

of his namesake, Joseph in Egypt, who also saved his family by taking them to Egypt. The newborn Jesus is the true King of Israel, to be sure, but he was also a new Moses, and Matthew anticipates some of Jesus' later ministry here in his Infancy Narrative. Because of Matthew's identification of Jesus with Moses, his depiction of Herod contains many echoes of Pharaoh, the wicked king of Egypt who also ordered the death of Israelite baby boys and who later opposed Moses' ministry. It is in this context that we can best appreciate the importance of the Wise Men, the star they followed, the slaughter of the children of Bethlehem, and other aspects of Matthew's narrative.

THE STORY OF THE WISE MEN

Matthew's account of the annunciation to Joseph (Matthew 1:18–21) and his brief account of the birth and naming of Jesus (Matthew 1:24–25) do not provide any information about the timing or location of these events. Only with the opening of the second chapter of Matthew's Infancy Narrative do we learn that Jesus "was born in Bethlehem of Judæa in the days of Herod the king" (Matthew 2:1). The mention of both Bethlehem and Herod the Great (ruled 37–4 B.C.), however, does more than establish date and place. Because Bethlehem was the city of David and the place that Matthew understood would be the home of the Messiah, the true King is placed in opposition to Herod. Many Jews saw Herod as a usurper who had taken the position of king of the Jews with Roman approval and support. In addition to providing political tension, Herod's status as a half-Jewish Idumean, perhaps only superficially converted to Judaism, also highlights the dichotomy that existed between the House of Israel and the Gentiles.

This context is important for understanding the role of the Magi, or Wise Men, who are also introduced as this chapter opens: "Behold, there came wise men from the east to Jerusalem" (Matthew 2:1). Matthew provides no other details about these enigmatic characters, not their number, names, nationality, or clear place of origin. All he says is that they came from east of the Holy Land, and he describes them by using the Greek term *magoi*. While this word was used specifically for the priestly caste of religious experts in Persia, it was also used broadly in Greek to describe anyone with special knowledge, whether spiritual, astronomical, or revelatory. Although the term

Courtesy of Chad Emmett.

Ruins of the Herodium, a palace, strong fortress, and tomb built by Herod the Great twelve miles south of Jerusalem near Bethlehem.

became pejorative in Latin (the Romans saw *magi* as charlatans at best or dark magicians at worst),[1] there is no indication that Matthew uses the word that way. Their arrival in Jerusalem asking, "Where is he that is born King of the Jews? for we have seen his star in the east" (Matthew 2:2) seems at first to support the idea that these wise men might have been the type of astrologers that *magoi* were often reputed to be.

Early Christian speculation soon suggested various places of origin and later even names for the Magi, but from the earliest they were assumed to have been Gentiles. Hence, while much of Matthew 1 focuses on Jesus' Davidic heritage and hence his position as a Jew and a member of the House of Israel, the Magi in Matthew 2 can be seen as reflecting Jesus' role in being a blessing to all people. *Gentiles* in English comes from the Latin word for "nations," and hence is a translation of the Greek term *ethnē* and the Hebrew word *goyim*. Though only some of the House of Israel recognized and accepted Jesus, if the Magi were in fact Gentiles, then their seeking the newborn King suggests that others outside of Israel might actively seek Jesus. In this sense, the Wise Men anticipated the Gentiles who would later join the New Testament Church. Thus, just as the women in Jesus' genealogy indicated that outsiders had a part in the coming forth of Jesus, so do the Magi illustrate that God will accept all people who will hearken to Christ.

On the other hand, some Latter-day Saint authors have noted that the Magi were not necessarily brought to Jerusalem because of astronomical observation and certainly not through superstitions or false religious teachings. Because the Joseph Smith Translation of the Bible changes "King of the Jews" to "the Messiah of the Jews," the Magi appear to have been familiar with Jewish prophecy and scripture. The Jewish Diaspora, or scattering, had distributed Jews throughout the Near East, making it possible that the Wise Men were themselves Jewish or that they were at least religious Gentiles who had familiarized themselves with Jewish texts. Another possibility is that they were from among the scattered tribes of Israel. In this case they might have had some understanding of their former identity, but they may also have been assimilated and lost among their Gentile neighbors. Nevertheless, whether Gentile, Jew, or from the lost tribes of Israel, what is certain is that these men, who had the privilege of being witnesses of the newborn Jesus, were no doubt good men moved upon by the Spirit of God.[2]

Courtesy of Chad Emmett.

Bethlehem as seen from the Herodium. It is possible that Herod might have been staying there when the Magi visited him.

Britten's *A Ceremony of Carols*

In 1942, while noted twentieth-century composer Benjamin Britten (1913–1976) was returning to England by sea, he composed the earliest version of a collection of Christmas carols that later became his celebrated *A Ceremony of Carols*. While a relatively modern composer, Britten set to music a number of Middle English texts, many of which he drew from the anthology *The English Galaxy of Shorter Poems* by Gerald Bullett (1893–1958). The combination of these old texts together with music that consciously drew from older forms and employed a boys' choir does much to connect Britten's piece with earlier Christmas masterworks. The opening procession and closing recessional, for instance, are both modeled after medieval plainchant.[3]

A *Ceremony of Carols* is composed for a treble chorus and soloists and is accompanied only by a harp. Some of the movements, such as "There is no Rose," "That yongë child," and "As dew in Aprille," prominently feature Mary and her child, corresponding well with the narrative of Luke 2. However, at least two movements match the context of Matthew 2, with its focus on Jesus as the true King and the murderous opposition that his birth aroused. For instance, the triumphant second movement, "Wolcum Yole!" begins, "Wolcum be thou hevenè king" (Welcome, O thou Heavenly King). Likewise, the sixth movement, "This little Babe," takes its lyrics from a poem of Robert Southwell (circa 1561–1595), an English Catholic martyr, and sings of how Jesus had come to overturn Satan's power and overwhelm the forces arrayed against him:

> This little Babe so few days old,
> Is come to rifle Satan's fold;
> All hell doth at his presence quake,
> Though he himself for cold do shake;
> For in this weak, unarmèd wise
> The gates of hell he will surprise.

> His camp is pitched in a stall,
> His bulwark but a broken wall;
> The crib his trench, haystalks his stakes;
> Of shepherds he his muster makes;
> And thus, as sure his foe to wound,
> The angels' trumps alarum sound.

> With tears he fights and wins the field,
> His naked breast stands for a shield;
> His battering shot are babish cries,
> His arrows looks of weeping eyes,
> His martial ensigns Cold and Need,
> And feeble Flesh his warrior's steed.

> My soul, with Christ join thou in fight;
> Stick to the tents that he hath pight.
> Within his crib is surest ward;
> This little Babe will be thy guard.
> If thou wilt foil thy foes with joy,
> Then flit not from this heavenly Boy.[4]

While not overly familiar to an American audience today, *A Ceremony of Carols* holds a place in the succession of great musical masterworks for Christmas that began with Corelli and continued with figures such as Bach and Handel. Listening to it at Christmastime can do much to evoke the feelings of magic and mystery that surround the Christmas story.

Magi Journeying, by James Tissot.

Regardless of their actual identity and background, in Matthew's narrative the Magi appear as outsiders who are brought by the direct intervention of God. In their case, God's revelation occurred in the form of an astronomical phenomenon. While the Jews had the law and the prophets to bring them to Christ, the Wise Men were brought by the sight of the star "in the east" (Greek, *en tē anatolē*). Rather than suggesting where the Magi were when they saw the star, the word order in Greek makes it likely that the phrase *en tē anatolē* modifies the Greek term for *star*. Further, "in the east" can be better translated "at its rising," indicating that it was a morning star that appeared before the sun's own rising.[5] Since antiquity, many efforts have been made to identify or explain what this star was. Suggestions include the appearance of a comet, a striking planetary conjunction, or a supernova, all of which might create the impression of a new, different, or unusually bright star.[6] Others propose that the star cannot be explained scientifically, making it simply a miraculous occurrence or sign, perhaps even a representation of angelic ministers.[7] Indeed, in the ancient world, stars and other heavenly bodies were often considered to be celestial beings, in which case the star may have represented a heavenly messenger or guide to the Wise Men, much as the angel of the Lord had served the shepherds in Luke 2:9–15.

Harmonizing the Infancy Narratives of Matthew and Luke often leads us to assume that this star could have been seen by everyone, an impulse perhaps encouraged by the fact that the celestial signs of Jesus' birth in the New World, including a "new" star, were seen by many there (Helaman 14:3–6; 3 Nephi 1:15, 19–21; see Chapter 5: Further Glad Tidings). Luke, however, never mentions the star of Bethlehem, nor does he suggest that the shepherds saw it. Likewise, there is not any indication in Matthew's text that Herod, his scribes, or the general populace in Judea had seen or noticed the star.[8] As a result, it is possible that in the Old World the sign of the star was one intended for those who knew what to look for,[9] unlike the western hemisphere, where it was intended as a sign for all. Also, Matthew's narrative does not indicate that the star was constantly visible even to the Magi. He simply states that the Wise Men had seen the star at its rising, and only later, after they had visited Herod in Jerusalem, did it return and seemingly lead them to Bethlehem, where it marked the place where Jesus was (Matthew 2:2, 9).

Whatever the star might have been, its symbolism had been anticipated in Old Testament prophecy, particularly in Numbers 24:17. There Balaam, a so-called prophet engaged by the king of Moab to curse Israel, instead repeatedly blesses God's people, ultimately prophesying that "there shall come a Star out of Jacob, and a Sceptre shall rise out of Israel." This prophecy took on strong messianic implications both before and after the New Testament.[10] That Jesus could be described as a star at its rising is clear from Revelation 22:16, where the resurrected and glorified Jesus describes himself as "the bright and morn-

ing star." Likewise, the prophet Isaiah proclaimed, "Arise, shine; for *thy light is come,* and the glory of the Lord *is risen* upon thee" (Isaiah 60:1; emphasis added). But the light of the star did not come only for the House of Israel. As two biblical scholars have observed, "The story of the star does not make a statement about an astronomical phenomenon, but a statement about Jesus: his birth is the coming of the light that draws wise men of the Gentiles to its radiance."[11] While the Magi represent those who recognize and seek this light, in contrast, Herod and his priestly and scribal ministers fail either to see the star or to realize its significance.[12]

Knowing through revelation,

Adoration of the Magi, by Giotto di Bondone.

confirmed by the sign of the star, that the true King of the Jews had been born, the Wise Men travel to Jerusalem, where they expected to find the new king. When they announce the purpose of their visit to the current king, Herod is troubled—"and all Jerusalem with him" (Matthew 2:3). Obviously Herod would be disturbed by the prospect of a new king replacing him, but the concern of the establishment in Jerusalem also anticipates the later opposition to Jesus from the chief priests, scribes, and other leadership in the Passion Narratives.[13] When Herod asks the chief priests and scribes where

Christmas Stars, Lights, and Trees

The star that the Magi saw in the east and then followed from Jerusalem to Bethlehem has become a central fixture in Christmas decorations today. Appearing atop Christmas trees, on presents, cards, and even in the shape of cookies, the star reminds us not only of the star that led the Magi but also that Christmas celebrates the coming of the true Light into a world of darkness. Because of that imagery, festive star-inspired lights brighten homes and hearts in the Christmas season.

The tradition of a Christmas tree has no biblical precedent, and it probably finds its antecedent in the evergreens—leaves, boughs, and even whole trees—that were used during the midwinter festivals of various cultures. However, because evergreens so powerfully symbolize the principle of eternal life, and perhaps because of a symbolic resonance with the Tree of Life, Christmas tree symbolism was easily co-opted by Christianity, maybe as early as A.D. 720, when St. Boniface is said to have replaced the sacred oak of the pagan Germans with a young fir tree.

Exactly how trees and lights came together is not clear. An unsubstantiated legend holds that one night during the Christmas season, circa 1530, Martin Luther was walking home through the forest. Seeing the stars gleaming around and above a fir tree, he was struck by its beauty and decided to decorate a tree in his home to recreate the effect. The earliest documented tree decorated with candles, however, dates almost a century later, in 1616. The custom of a lighted and decorated tree traveled from Germany to England when Prince Albert started the tradition of setting one up at Windsor Castle. When an engraving of the royal family around a Christmas tree was published in 1848, the practice spread throughout England, from there to America, and then throughout the world.[14]

Christmas lights and other ornaments decorate Christmas trees, joining the symbols of eternal life and Christ as the light of the world.

How the Wise Men Became Kings

Matthew uses the term *magoi* for the special visitors who come to the child Jesus bearing gifts of gold, frankincense, and myrrh. Nowhere does he number them, but because he speaks of wise men in the plural, there must have been two or more. Early artistic representations depict two, three, four, even as many as twelve wise men visiting the mother and child. The number three seems to have become established because of the number of gifts that they brought.

More interesting is how the Magi came to be viewed as kings. The possibility of their being royalty might have been suggested by their wealth, because the gifts they presented to Jesus were worthy of a king. But early Christians seem to have made the connection with royalty as they reflected upon certain Old Testament passages, such as Psalm 69:29 and 72:10, which suggest that kings from among the nations would come to Israel bearing gifts. Particularly significant were passages from the prophet Isaiah. Connecting the coming of kings with the light of a rising star, Isaiah 60:3 prophesies, "And the Gentiles shall come to thy light, and kings to the brightness of thy rising." A few verses later some of their gifts and even the camels that were later assumed to be their conveyance are mentioned: "The multitude of camels shall cover thee, the dromedaries of Midian and Ephah; all they from Sheba shall come: they shall bring gold and incense; and they shall shew forth the praises of the Lord" (Isaiah 60:6).[15]

Courtesy of Bridgeman Art Library. Used by permission.

In the church of Saint Apollinare Nuovo in Ravenna is a sixth-century Byzantine mosaic depicting the three Magi bringing their gifts to the Baby Jesus.

While the various Eastern churches produced a variety of names for the wise men, by the third century the Western tradition had established the names Gaspar, Balthasar, and Melchior for the kings. Eventually each of the three was associated with a different continent and people, symbolic of all the nations of the earth honoring Jesus.[16]

Christ, or the Messiah, should be born, their response provides Matthew with his second explicitly fulfilled prophecy, "And thou Bethlehem, in the land of Juda, art not the least among the princes of Juda: for out of thee shall come a Governor, that shall rule my people Israel" (Matthew 2:6; JST, Matthew 3:6 changes "Governor" to "prince" to emphasize Jesus' royal status). This passage mostly echoes Micah 5:2, but it also echoes 2 Samuel 5:2, where David was anointed king of all Israel.[17] John 7:42 confirms that at the time of Jesus, Bethlehem was known to be the place from which the Messiah would come. In this passage, those opposing the adult Jesus as he spoke in the temple during the feast of Tabernacles ask themselves, "Hath not the scripture said, That Christ cometh of the seed of David, and out of the town of Bethlehem, where David was?" This reference to Bethlehem not only corroborates Jesus' Davidic heritage but it also underscores that Herod, the then-current king in Jerusalem,

"What Shall We Give to the Babe in the Manger?"

In 2001, Mack Wilberg, then associate director of the Mormon Tabernacle Choir, published a setting of a traditional Catalonian carol with an English paraphrase by David Warner.[18] The lyrics by Warner movingly connect the visit of the Wise Men at Jesus' birth to the rest of the Savior's ministry and with his saving death and Resurrection.

The first verse finds us with the Magi approaching the Baby, wondering what an appropriate gift should be. The second verse moves through Jesus' boyhood and ministry, seeing him as the boy in the temple and the man teaching and working miracles by the Sea of Galilee. The verse concludes with Jesus entering Jerusalem on Palm Sunday before carrying his cross on Good Friday. Following a reflection on his Resurrection in the third verse, the song resolves that the only fitting gift that any of us can give the Savior are tears for his mercy and love.

What shall we give to the Babe in the manger?
What shall we offer the Child in the stall?
Incense and spices and gold we've a-plenty.
Are these the gifts for the King of us all?

What shall we give to the Boy in the temple?
What shall we offer the Man by the sea?

Palms at His feet and hosannas uprising,
Are these for Him who will carry the tree?

What shall we give to the Lamb who was offered,
Rising the third day and shedding His Love?
Tears for His mercy we'll weep at the manger,
Bathing the Infant come down from above.[19]

"What Shall We Give to the Babe in the Manger?" thus illustrates beautifully through music what President Gordon B. Hinckley wrote in his December 2000 Christmas message: "There would be no Christmas if there had not been Easter. The babe Jesus of Bethlehem would be but another baby without the redeeming Christ of Gethsemane and Calvary, and the triumphant fact of the Resurrection."[20]

Giving Gifts at Christmastime

The gifts of gold, frankincense, and myrrh offered by the Wise Men to Jesus have served through the centuries as a precedent for the giving of gifts at Christmas. Today we are moved to give gifts—both presents of worldly things and also gifts of the heart—to those whom we love at this special season. While we often lose sight of the true purpose of giving, Jesus' teaching that "inasmuch as ye have done it unto one of the least of these my brethren, ye have done it unto me" (Matthew 25:40) implicitly suggests that when we love, serve, and give to those whom Christ loves, we are, in fact, giving to him.

In some cultures, the example of the Wise Men is remembered on January 6, or Epiphany, which is celebrated as "Three Kings' Day." On this occasion children often receive candy and toys in their shoes, which are left out the night before.[21] But a larger influence on the tradition of giving gifts at the Christmas season was the legend of St. Nicholas of Myra, a fourth-century bishop in a Roman town in Asia Minor, in what is now Turkey. Although no evidence about Nicholas has survived from the time in which he lived, in the Middle Ages stories circulated about his famous kindness and generosity. Because he reputedly saved three young girls by secretly giving them bags of gold, his example became the model for anonymous giving, in line with the Savior's injunction, "But when thou doest alms, let not thy left hand know what thy right hand doeth" (Matthew 6:3). Nicholas also became the patron saint of children, and when his relics were moved to Bari in Italy in 1087, he and his story became part of Western European culture. Thus his feast day on December 6 became the customary day to give gifts to children, and by the sixteenth century, German children were hanging their stockings out on the eve of his feast day for him to fill with presents as he had given bags of gold to the girls at Myra.

The Protestant Reformation disapproved of the veneration of saints, so Martin Luther encouraged another incarnation of the spirit of giving in the form of the *Christkindl*, or "Christ Child." Also known as Kris Kringle, this figure gave gifts on either December 25 or New Year's Day, rather than on St. Nicholas's feast day. Likewise,

The sap or resin flowing from the frankincense tree was, and still is, used to make incense.

Courtesy of Chad Emmett.

Henry VIII is said to have introduced a figure known as Father Christmas in England. The Dutch continued the tradition of St. Nicholas in the form of *Sinterklaas*, bringing him to New Amsterdam, later known as New York. Through the writings of Washington Irving in 1809 and an anonymous 1823 poem called "A Visit from St. Nicholas" (later known as "The Night before Christmas" and attributed to Clement Clarke Moore), Santa Claus became an important fixture in American Christmases, from where that tradition has spread around the world.[22]

While we continue to give gifts to our loved ones openly at Christmastime and receive them in turn, there is something about the spirit of Santa Claus that continues to reflect and add to the joy of the Christmas season. As famously expressed in a *New York Sun* editorial on September 21, 1897: "Yes, Virginia, there is a Santa Claus. He exists as certainly as love and generosity and devotion exist, and you know that they abound and give to your life its highest beauty and joy. . . . He lives and lives forever. A thousand years from now, Virginia, nay, 10 times 10,000 years from now, he will continue to make glad the heart of childhood."[23] Similarly, Latter-day Saint storyteller George Durrant wrote: "There really is a Santa Claus. A Santa who knows that one of the happiest things we can do at Christmastime is to give something to someone without telling him who gave it. . . . A Santa who enjoys getting the blame for things that make Christmas a time for little ones to have a full measure of Christmas joy."[24]

But in the midst of both known and anonymous gift-giving at Christmastime, for believers, the ultimate gift remains the tidings of great joy that come from knowing that God gave us his Son at Christmastime—and that Christ loved us so much that he suffered and gave his life for us.

was illegitimate. While David had come from Bethlehem, he and his successors ruled from Jerusalem. Because Herod had no real right to rule, a new king needed to come from the place where David himself had been born.

Under the pretense of wanting to honor the child, Herod sends the Wise Men ahead to Bethlehem to find the new King. But it is not the direction provided by Herod and his priests that brings the Magi to Jesus. Instead, as soon as they leave Jerusalem, the miraculous star reappears and guides them. Significantly, upon seeing its return, "they rejoiced with exceeding *great joy*" (Greek, *charan megalēn;* Matthew 2:10; emphasis added). Luke uses these same words when reporting the angel's "good tidings of *great joy*" (Luke 2:10; emphasis added), effectively equating the star with the angel of the Lord, each being a celestial messenger bringing good news to those prepared or chosen to receive it. While most scholars maintain that Matthew would not have known Luke's text, the fact that they use the same Greek words for "great joy" suggests the importance of the theme of joy to the stories surrounding Jesus' birth.

In Bethlehem, the Wise Men find the child Jesus and his mother, Mary, not in a cave, stable, other animal quarters, or in temporary accommodations. Instead, they find him in a house (Matthew 2:11), indicating that the Wise Men arrived much later than the shepherds did when they found the baby in the manger. In fact, their arrival may have been as much as two years after Jesus' birth, because two is the age that Herod uses as his upper limit when he orders the slaughter of the children in Bethlehem. In a scene known in art as the Adoration of the Magi, the Wise Men upon their arrival fall before the child and worship him, honoring him even more explicitly than the shepherds did in Luke's account. They present him with three treasures—gold, frankincense, and myrrh—which were symbolic as well as valuable. Gold, of course, was fit for a king. Frankincense was used in worship, and it alludes to Jesus' future priestly role as both the sacrificer and the sacrifice. Myrrh, often used to anoint bodies for burial, foreshadows his future sacrificial death.[25] Warned in a dream by the angel of the Lord not to return to Herod, the Magi return home by another route, disappearing from history but not from our Christmas imagination.

The Escape into Egypt and The Massacre of the Innocents

That the Wise Men were warned in a revelatory dream not only supports the idea that they were righteous, inspired men but it also reintroduces the figure of Joseph the Carpenter, who had not been specifically mentioned in Matthew 2:1–12. Joseph's own ability to be guided through revelation or inspired dreams had been established in Matthew 1:20–25, and he receives three other such revelatory dreams in Matthew 2, associating him closely with his namesake, Joseph in Egypt, who was both a dreamer and an interpreter of dreams—and one who saved his family from death by bringing them to Egypt. In the case of the Joseph in Genesis, death threatened in the face of famine; in the case of Matthew's Joseph, the threat comes in the form of Herod, who tries to destroy his perceived rival

Anno Domini (Flight into Egypt), *by Edwin Longsden Long.*

A rural scene outside of Luxor in Egypt.

(Matthew 2:13). Obedient to the direction he received, Joseph arises during the night and, taking Jesus and Mary, travels with them to Egypt (Matthew 2:14).

Because of its proximity, Egypt was a frequent sanctuary for those in the southern part of the Holy Land who faced famine, political threats, or invasions. Before Jacob and his sons, Abraham himself sojourned in the land of the Nile River valley. Later in Old Testament history, Jeroboam fled to Egypt when Solomon, seeing him as a potential rival, tried to kill him (1 Kings 11:40). After the Babylonian sack of Jerusalem, Jewish refugees took Jeremiah with them when they sought refuge in Egypt (Jeremiah 43:4–7). Accordingly, the angel's direction to Joseph to flee into Egypt, out of Herod's jurisdiction, not only made good practical sense but also laid the groundwork for another prophecy fulfillment, because if he went to Egypt, then he would one day return.

Matthew cites Hosea 11:1 in his familiar formula quotation pattern, "And he was there until the death of Herod: that it might be fulfilled which was spoken of the Lord by the prophet, saying, Out of Egypt have I called my son" (Matthew 2:15). In the original context of Hosea, the reference to God's son seems to refer to the Exodus, something that the compilers of the Septuagint tried to clarify by rendering "son" as "children" (Greek, *tekna*). But Matthew, though writing his quotation in Greek, stayed closer to the Hebrew original,[26] seeing the Hosea passage as ultimately being fulfilled when God called his Only Begotten Son out of Egypt and back to Israel once Herod dies.

The sun sets over the Nile River in Egypt.

The connection between God's son seen as the house of Israel and Jesus as his actual Son introduces an important motif in Matthew's Gospel, namely the idea that Jesus' life echoes many of the experiences of the house of Israel throughout its history. For instance, after Jesus' baptism (Matthew 3:14–16), he is led into the desert for forty days (Matthew 4:1–11), reenacting in a sense the forty-year wandering of Israel in the wilderness after crossing the Red Sea. More personally, Jesus' life and ministry is shown to have been anticipated in many ways by Moses' life and ministry. Moses was to be Israel's deliverer, and the miraculous acts he wrought, through which the Lord delivered the children of Israel from slavery and the angel of death, were types of how Jesus delivers us from the bondage of sin and physical death. Likewise, God gave through Moses both the law and manna from heaven, just as Jesus fulfilled the law through his Sermon on the Mount and, as the true Bread of Life, through his atoning sacrifice.

Massacre of the Innocents, *by James Tissot.*

Such parallels with Moses also help explain some of the significance of Herod's next vicious act. Angry that the Wise Men eluded him and did not bring him detailed information about the newborn king, Herod resolves to kill all the children under the age of two in and around Bethlehem (Matthew 2:16). While the KJV reads "children," the Greek text uses *tous paidous,* a masculine plural form that suggests male children. While it is possible that this is a collective term that might also include female children, the image of a wicked king killing male children resonates with the account of Pharaoh killing the sons born to the Hebrews in Goshen (Exodus 1:22). While that is as much detail as the Old Testament gives, expansions of Moses' story circulating at the time of Matthew explained that one of the reasons Pharaoh killed the Israelite baby boys was to destroy the promised deliverer before he could grow up and free his people[27]—just as Herod tried to kill the actual Deliverer before he could, as Messiah, take Herod's throne.

The terrible slaughter of the children in Bethlehem has come to be known as the Massacre of the Innocents, depicted movingly in art and even in song. While this story looms large in our memory of the events surrounding the birth of Jesus, surprisingly, Josephus—the major source for Jewish history of this period who documented many of Herod's other, well-known atrocities—makes no mention of a massacre in Bethlehem. Nor is it well-attested in other ancient sources.[28] This may be because, though later Christian writers put the number of innocent children killed as high as 64,000, the actual number of children killed may have been relatively small.[29] If Bethlehem were a small town of about 1,000 permanent residents, birthrates and other demographic factors combine to suggest a number as low as twenty. While it was an unbearable tragedy for the families involved, the deaths of twenty children from largely unknown families would not necessarily have been noted in secular histories.

Matthew uses the grief the families must have felt as the catalyst for his fourth formula quotation, which states, "Then was fulfilled that which was spoken by Jeremy the prophet, saying, In Rama was there a voice heard, lamentation, and weeping, and great mourning, Rachel weeping for her children, and would not be comforted, because they are not" (Matthew 2:17–18). Here Matthew cites Jeremiah 31:15, which in its original context had reference to either the destruction of the northern kingdom of Israel in 721 B.C. or the devastation of northern Judah in Jeremiah's own time, either 597 or 587 B.C. Rachel's descendants in the tribes of Manasseh and Ephraim were prominent in the northern kingdom, and the tribe of Benjamin in northern Judah likewise was descended from her. Rama, just north of Jerusalem in the territory of Benjamin, is suggested as the burial site of the matriarch Rachel in 1 Samuel 10:2. This site was also the point of deportation for her children from the tribe of Benjamin during the Babylonian captivity. By Matthew's time, however, the tomb of Rachel was believed to have been near Bethlehem, allowing Matthew to imagine the matriarch weeping with the women of Bethlehem in their terrible grief. Known today as *Kever Rakhel* in Hebrew and *Qubbat Rahil* in Arabic, it remains an important shrine to both Jews and Muslims.[30]

None of the children of Bethlehem, or at least very few of them, were likely to have been actual descendants of Rachel. But the image of Jeremiah's Rachel weeping for her children as they went off into exile injects an element of hope into the story of the Massacre of the Innocents, because the exile of these tribes came with a promise of their eventual restoration.[31] Likewise, through Christ, those lost to death are promised resurrection, and the truly innocent, like these children who were under the age of accountability, are guaranteed a glorious resurrection and eternal life.

Courtesy of D. Kelly Ogden.

The traditional site of Rachel's Tomb outside of Bethlehem.

"Coventry Carol"

This moving carol is one of few surviving pieces from a medieval cycle of mystery plays that was produced every year by the Shearman and Tailors' Guild in Coventry, England. In addition to usual Christmas stories such as the Annunciation, the Nativity, and the Adoration of the Magi, the guild also produced a scene about the Massacre of the Innocents. A certain Robert Croo wrote some or all of the play, and hence the lyrics to this song, in 1534. The haunting music to which it is now sung was edited and published by Thomas Sharp in 1825.

In this carol, the women of Bethlehem sing to their children, trying to keep them quiet so that the soldiers of King Herod do not hear them. But the raging king orders his soldiers onward, and in the fourth and final verse the women bewail the death of their children.[32]

Lullay, Thou little tiny Child,
By, by, lully, lullay.
Lullay, Thou little tiny Child,
By, by, lully, lullay.

O sisters too, how may we do,
For to preserve this day?
This poor youngling for whom we sing,
"By, by, lully, lullay."

Herod the king, in his raging,
Charged he hath this day.
His men of might, in his own sight,
All young children to slay.

That woe is me, poor child for Thee!
And ever mourn and say,
For thy parting neither say nor sing,
"By, by, lully, lullay."[33]

The "Return" to Nazareth

When Herod died, and the immediate threat to Jesus' life was over, the angel of the Lord appeared to Joseph yet again in a dream. As before, the Joseph Smith Translation changes "dream" to "vision," indicating that the message was a true revelation, either in an open vision or, as I have suggested, emphasizing that it was a revelatory dream. In Joseph's vision, the angel bids him to take the child and Mary back to the land of Israel, noting "for *they* are dead which sought the young child's life" (Matthew 2:20; emphasis added). This directive recalls the command of the Lord to Moses when he bade that Moses return to Egypt from his refuge in Midian, "Go, return into Egypt: for all the men are dead which sought thy life" (Exodus 4:19).

While the close verbal parallel alludes to the comparison between Jesus and Moses, using the plural "they" also suggests that others had colluded with Herod in trying to kill the newborn King. The likely culprits are the chief priests and scribes of Jerusalem, who had been troubled along with Herod at news from the Magi that a new King of the Jews had been born.[34] This arraying of the political and religious establishment against the young Jesus anticipates the alliance of the chief priests and scribes with Pilate against the adult Christ in the Passion Narrative at the end of Matthew's Gospel, once again connecting Christmas to the story of Easter.

Upon the death of Herod the Great, his kingdom was divided among three of his sons. One, Herod Archelaus, received Samaria, Judea, and Idumea, while Herod Antipas received Galilee and Perea (territory across the Jordan River), and Herod Philip received territory in the northeastern part of the Holy Land. Archelaus received the title ethnarch, or "ruler of the people," and Antipas and Philip the lesser titles of tetrarch, or "rulers of a fourth part."[35] Because Archelaus received the largest portion, including the capital, Jerusalem, Matthew speaks of him "ruling in place of his father Herod" (NIV, Matthew 2:22; KJV, "reign[ing] in Judaea in the room of his father Herod"). Josephus records that Archelaus was a violent and tyrannical ruler, so much so that after ten years the upper classes of Jerusalem petitioned the Romans to depose him, accepting a Roman governor rather than another unstable Herodian ruler.[36]

Apparently Joseph had planned to return to Bethlehem from Egypt, either because Bethlehem had always been his home or because Bethlehem was where he and Mary had obtained a house in the first years of Jesus' life. However, knowing Archelaus' unstable nature and how violent his rule would

Courtesy of Bridgeman Art Library. Used by permission.

Return from Egypt, *by James Tissot.*

Sadness at Christmastime

The grief of the mothers of Bethlehem compels us to face a sad reality: what is such a joyous season for so many is often a cheerless and even depressing time for others. As Elder Jeffrey R. Holland has written, "For many people in many places this may not be an entirely happy Christmas, one not filled with complete joy because of the circumstances facing a spouse or a friend, a child or a grandchild. Or perhaps that was the case another Christmas in another year, but one which brings a painful annual memory to us yet."[37] To the list of those who have lost a loved one or suffered some personal pain, I would add those who are alone, ill, or chronically depressed at Christmastime. Circumstances beyond our control often weigh heavily upon us, set in sharp contrast by the seeming joy of so many around us. And sometimes the sadness we feel is simply the regret and letdown that comes when a happy time comes to a necessary end, and we are confronted with the resumption of the dreary routine of day-to-day living.

In his short book, *Shepherds Why This Jubilee?* Elder Holland concludes by reflecting on a sad Christmas in his own life, recounting the year his father suffered a heart attack following surgery just before Christmas. Early Christmas morning in 1976, at the hospital, facing the imminent loss of his father, the sound of a newborn baby jolted him out of his sorrow. Comparing the joy of that baby's parents to that of Mary and Joseph that first Christmas, Elder Holland considered the great plan of salvation that the Babe of Bethlehem, as the Man on the Cross, would effect for us. He wrote: "Temporary separation at death and the other difficulties that attend us as we all move toward that end are part of the price we pay for . . . birth and family ties and the fun of Christmas together. . . . These are God's gifts to us—birth and life and death and salvation, the whole divine experience in all its richness and complexity."[38]

Christmas may not always be happy. But the coming of Jesus into the world that wonderful night made possible the great Atonement, death, and Resurrection of our Lord, which are the true tidings of great joy. Hopefully we can ameliorate our own sadness by serving and giving to others, lightening their burdens, and easing their loneliness. Ultimately, however, we must faithfully lay hold on the promise that joy—true joy without end—lies ahead.

prove to be, the Lord once again inspired Joseph, directing him in a dream to go instead to Galilee (Matthew 2:22), where the administration of Herod Antipas was less dangerous for the family. Joseph chose to settle his family in Nazareth, the town where Mary was from (Luke 1:26–27; 1 Nephi 11:13). Harmonies of the Infancy Narratives assume that Joseph was also from Nazareth. While this is certainly possible, taken by itself Matthew's account seems to imply that Joseph was from Bethlehem all along (see Chapter 2: Promised Savior). In this case, it was not a "return" to Nazareth as much as it was relocating to a village where Mary's relatives could help establish the family in a new home.

Joseph's moving his family to Nazareth occasions Matthew's fifth and final formula quotation

Courtesy of Chad Emmett.

Modern Nazareth in Galilee.

in his Infancy Narrative: "And he came and dwelt in a city called Nazareth: that it might be fulfilled which was spoken by the prophets, He shall be called *a Nazarene*" (Matthew 2:23; emphasis added). It is not clear which prophet or prophets Matthew might be citing here, but the term "Nazarene" (Greek, *Nazōraios*) may provide a clue. On its most obvious level, being a Nazarene means being from Nazareth, and John reports that Jesus was called "Jesus of Nazareth" on the title affixed to his cross (John 19:19). Nazareth is never mentioned in the Old Testament, however, and there are not any surviving prophecies stating that the Messiah would be from there. Two separate Hebrew words, however, are similar to this Greek transliteration, and Matthew might have had one or both of them in mind when he wrote *Nazōraios*. First, the Hebrew term for a Nazarite—one dedicated to God's service by a special vow—is *nāzîr*. Suggesting that Jesus would be a Nazarite evokes echoes with Judges 13:2–7, which describes Samson as a Nazarite from birth, and 1 Samuel 1:11 and 22, which suggest that the boy Samuel would also be a Nazarite.[39] Second, the Hebrew word *nēṣer*, or "branch," appears in Isaiah 11:1: "And there shall come forth a rod out of the stem of Jesse, and *a Branch* shall grow out of his roots" (emphasis added).[40]

THE CONCLUSION OF MATTHEW'S STORY

The received text of Matthew does not present as clear a conclusion to his Infancy Narrative as Luke's does with Luke's notice that "the child grew, and waxed strong in spirit, filled with wisdom: and the grace of God was upon him" (Luke 2:40). The Joseph Smith Translation, however, provides a final verse that parallels Luke's ending: "And it came to pass that Jesus grew up with his brethren, and waxed strong, and waited upon the Lord for the time of his ministry to come" (JST, Matthew 3:24). This expansion is followed by two more verses that complement Luke's story of the boy Jesus in the temple (see Conclusion: Remembering Christmas), but the ending as we have it, which closes with the formula quotation about Jesus being a Nazarene, may present a fitting conclusion in itself. By implying two important things about this Son of David and King of Israel—namely, that he was holy and fully consecrated to God's service and that he was, in fact, the Righteous Branch of the House of David—Matthew leaves us with a true understanding of *who* Jesus was and *how* his life would be lived. Like the Magi, we are enjoined to be wise men and women, called to seek Jesus Christ with the promise that God will reveal and confirm these glad tidings in our own hearts. ❖

THE ADVENT THEME OF PEACE

Matthew 2 juxtaposes temporal rulers—Herod, his son Archelaus, and, by implication, even Pharaoh of Egypt—with the Babe of Bethlehem. In contrast to these violent, even murderous rulers, the true King of Israel was to be the "Prince of Peace" (Isaiah 9:6). However, the peace that Jesus brings is as often internal and spiritual as it is external and temporal. While the prophecies of Isaiah describe the era of world peace that Christ will establish in the Millennium, the joyful message of both Christmas and Easter is that we can have peace in this life *now*, regardless of the earthly circumstances in which we might find ourselves. Through Jesus Christ, we can be reconciled to God, having peace of conscience and the quiet, strengthening support of his Spirit in times of trouble and heartache. Once we are at peace with God, we can then work, heart by heart, at being at peace with those around us.

In the New Testament, Paul describes "the peace of God, which passeth all understanding" (Philippians 4:7), and in the Doctrine and Covenants we are promised that we can have "peace in this world" as well as "eternal life in the world to come" (D&C 59:23). Accordingly, on the last Sunday of Advent, the last Sunday before Christmas itself, we celebrate the peace that the birth of Jesus promised and the Atonement of Jesus accomplished. Some scriptures about the peace of Christ that reflect this Advent theme include the following:

Courtesy of Eric Huntsman.

The last purple candle celebrates the peace that Jesus brings into the world. With the fourth Sunday of Advent, all the outer candles are lit.

"And there shall come forth a rod out of the stem of Jesse, and a Branch shall grow out of his roots: And the spirit of the Lord shall rest upon him, the spirit of wisdom and understanding, the spirit of counsel and might, the spirit of knowledge and of the fear of the Lord; and shall make him of quick understanding in the fear of the Lord: and he shall not judge after the sight of his eyes, neither reprove after the hearing of his ears: *But with righteousness shall he judge the poor, and reprove with equity for the meek of the earth.* . . .

"*The wolf also shall dwell with the lamb,* and the leopard shall lie down with the kid; and the calf and the young lion and the fatling together; and a little child shall lead them. And the cow and the bear shall feed; their young ones shall lie down together: and the lion shall eat straw like the ox. And the sucking child shall play on the hole of the asp, and the weaned child shall put his hand on the cockatrice's den. *They shall not hurt nor destroy in all my holy mountain:* for the earth shall be full of the knowledge of the Lord, as the waters cover the sea. And in that day there shall be a root of Jesse, which shall stand for an ensign of the people; to it shall the Gentiles seek: and *his rest shall be glorious*" (Isaiah 11:1–4, 6–10; emphasis added).

"And behold, I say unto you, this is not all. For O how beautiful upon the mountains are the feet *of him that bringeth good tidings, that is the founder of peace,* yea, even the Lord, who has redeemed his people; yea, him who has granted salvation unto his people; for were it not for the redemption which he hath made for his people, which was prepared from the foundation of the world, I say unto you, were it not for this, all mankind must have perished. But behold, the bands of death shall be broken, and the Son reigneth, and hath power over the dead; therefore, he bringeth to pass the resurrection of the dead" (Mosiah 15:18–20; emphasis added).

"*Peace I leave with you, my peace I give unto you:* not as the world giveth, give I unto you. Let not your heart be troubled, neither let it be afraid" (John 14:27; emphasis added).

If a family celebration of Advent includes recalling the covenants that God has made with his people through the generations, the fourth candle can also be used to remember the covenant that the Lord made with David, namely that in his line there would always be a king in Israel. This promise has received its glorious and final fulfillment in Jesus Christ, who as King of Kings and Lord of Lords will establish peace in our hearts, in our homes, and, one day, throughout all the world.

Rachel and Samuel on Christmas Eve.

Courtesy of Eric Huntsman.

A familiar carol whose lyrics reflect the peace we celebrate at Christmastime is "It Came upon the Midnight Clear." Written in 1859 by Edmund Hamilton Sears (1810–1876) and set to a tune by Richard Storrs Willis (1819–1900), the original version of this carol consisted of five verses, although frequently, as in the LDS hymnal, only three are sung.[1] Its first verse reflects the sentiment of the angel's proclamation in Luke 2:14 with a paraphrase, "peace on the earth, good will to men." Likewise, the familiar version of the final verse speaks of the future time "when the new heaven and earth shall own the Prince of Peace their king." The less-frequently sung third and fourth verses reflect on how men so often refuse to hear the message of peace that the angels sang that first Christmas night. Their description of a world overwhelmed by sin, strife, and personal challenges illustrates the desperate need for the peace that Jesus brings, calling upon us to hush the noise of this world's strife and find rest:

Yet with the woes of sin and strife
The world has suffered long:
Beneath the angels' strain have rolled
Two thousand years of wrong,
And man, at war with man, hears not
The love-song which they bring:
O hush the noise, ye men of strife,
And hear the angels sing!

And ye, beneath life's crushing load,
Whose forms are bending low,
Who toil along the climbing way
With painful steps and slow,
Look now! for glad and golden hours
Come swiftly on the wing;
O rest beside the weary road,
And hear the angels sing![2]

5
FURTHER GLAD TIDINGS

A Book of Mormon Christmas

I am come to declare unto you the glad tidings of great joy. . . . For behold, the time cometh [when] the Lord Omnipotent who reigneth . . . shall come down from heaven. . . . And lo, he shall suffer temptations, and pain . . . even more than man can suffer . . . for behold, blood cometh from every pore, so great shall be his anguish.

—Mosiah 3:3–7

The Infancy Narratives of Matthew and Luke provide two substantially different stories of the divine conception and miraculous birth of Jesus. Nevertheless, while it is not always easy to harmonize the two accounts, focusing on their differences can detract from the joy that should attend the celebration of the Christmas story. I have found that a better approach is to study them separately, appreciating the unique contributions and insights of each author, seeing how the stories they tell set the stage for their particular Gospel. Then, by focusing on the major points they have in common, we can see them as complementary, with both stories agreeing on certain fundamental points while separately filling in aspects of the larger story not found in the other. Both accounts testify of the same basic truths: the coming of Jesus Christ into the world was long-prophesied; his mother, Mary, was a pure and chosen vessel; his conception was both miraculous and divine; and his birth was attended by heavenly and earthly witnesses. Above all, who Jesus was and would be and what he came to do constitute the "good tidings of great joy" intended for all people (Luke 2:10): this Babe of Bethlehem was the Promised Savior, whose atoning sacrifice, death, and Resurrection brought salvation.

Latter-day Saints find important confirmation and explication of these vital truths in Book of Mormon prophecies, which provide further "glad tidings of great joy" (Mosiah 3:3; Alma 13:22; Helaman 16:14; see also Alma 13:23; 39:15–19; Helaman 13:7; 3 Nephi 1:26). As another testament of Jesus Christ, this volume of restoration scripture corroborates the fundamental details of the story of Jesus' birth. But perhaps more importantly, Book of Mormon passages provide expanded understanding of exactly

Christ in Gethsemane, altarpiece by Carl Bloch. Courtesy Hope Gallery. King Benjamin taught that Christ would suffer for his people.

> ## Glad Tidings from the Book of Mormon
>
> • Nephi's Vision (1 Nephi 11:12–33)
> • King Benjamin's Story (Mosiah 3:1–13)
> • Abinadi's Sermon (Mosiah 15:1–31)
> • Alma's Testimony (Alma 7:9–14)
> • Samuel the Lamanite's Prophecy (Helaman 14:1–8)
> • Nephi the Son of Nephi's Story (3 Nephi 1:1–21)

Robert Cundick's *Redeemer*

In 1977, Latter-day Saint composer Robert M. Cundick (1926–) collaborated with Brigham Young University professor Ralph Woodward (1918–2005) in producing *The Redeemer*, a full-length oratorio in the tradition of Handel's *Messiah*. Woodward selected scriptures from all four LDS standard works for a "musical service depicting the doctrines and Atonement of Jesus Christ" and then approached Cundick, who served as Tabernacle organist from April 1965 until December 1991, to compose the score. Brother Cundick created what can be considered an LDS masterwork, one that involves soloists, a large choir, and a full symphony orchestra. But because of the nature of the work, he preferred calling it a "sacred service of music" rather than an oratorio, requesting that its performances always begin and end with prayer.[1] Since its premier performance by the BYU Oratorio Choir and Philharmonic Orchestra on March 24, 1978, *The Redeemer* has served as a powerful musical testimony to both LDS performers and listeners for more than thirty years.

Spanning the prophesied coming of the Redeemer, the achievement of his atoning sacrifice, and the promise that it offers us, *The Redeemer*, like *Messiah*, is divided into three parts, with the first, entitled "The Prophecy," dealing with the promised coming of Jesus Christ. While the third movement in this part, "My Soul Doth Magnify the Lord," is a beautiful setting of Mary's *Magnificat* from the book of Luke for a soprano soloist, other movements in "The Prophecy" powerfully portray Book of Mormon prophecies concerning the coming of Jesus Christ into the world and his subsequent mission. These include a setting of the angel's words about the Savior's mission from 1 Nephi 11 in "I Saw the Heavens Opened"; Abinadi's sermon on Jesus' role as the Father and the Son from Mosiah 15 in "Because He Dwelleth in the Flesh"; and Alma's testimony from Alma 7 in "Behold! He Shall Be Born of Mary."[2]

The women of the Mormon Tabernacle Choir and the ringers of the Bells at Temple Square reflect the joy of the Christmas season.

who this promised Savior would be and help us realize that the "glad tidings" have more to do with what Jesus accomplished for us than they do about the understandable joy that surrounded his birth.[3] Indeed, the central Book of Mormon message focuses squarely on salvation, with prophecies about Jesus focusing more on his saving work than on his promised nativity.[4]

NEPHI'S VISION

Nephi was the recipient of a powerful vision that expanded upon the dream that his father, Lehi, had earlier received about the Tree of Life. This vision is one of the pivotal passages of the Book of Mormon, powerfully laying out the identity, coming forth, and Atonement of Jesus Christ.[5] Before this, Lehi had preached in Jerusalem and taught his family about "the coming of [the] Messiah" (1 Nephi 1:19; see 1 Nephi 10:4–10), but it was the symbolism of Lehi's dream (1 Nephi 8:5–33) that prompted Nephi to obtain a witness of his father's teaching for himself. While Nephi's vision contains all of the elements of his father's earlier dream, it also includes additional teaching by the Spirit and a direct angelic tutorial, which allowed him to learn and understand the meaning and significance of the most important symbols in the dream. Central to what Nephi learned was how the Son of God would come into the world and what his mission would be.

Before revealing these things to Nephi, the Spirit tells him that in addition to seeing the Tree of Life, he will see "a man descending out of heaven" (1 Nephi 11:7). Nephi is to become a witness of this figure and bear testimony that the man is "the Son of God" (1 Nephi 11:7). After Nephi sees the tree, the Spirit tells him to look, whereupon Nephi "beheld the city of Nazareth; and in the city of Nazareth I beheld a virgin, and she was exceedingly fair and white" (1 Nephi 11:13). An angel then appears and guides Nephi through the remainder of his vision. The angel asks Nephi a series of questions which help him understand the significance of the Son of God becoming flesh, what Mary's role was, and how the tree and other symbols represent Jesus and his role.

One of the first things the angel asks Nephi is whether he understands "the condescension of God" (1 Nephi 11:16). Whereas Matthew and Luke help their readers understand that Jesus was the Son of God because of his divine conception and miraculous birth, the angel in Nephi's vision uses the term *condescension* to teach a concept also known from the Gospel of John, namely that Jesus was divine even before his birth to Mary (John 1:1–2). Literally meaning "to come down" and "dwell with," *condescend* refers to a voluntary descent from one's status or dignity in order to relate to and help inferiors. While some Latter-day Saint commentators have observed that the first use of this term in 1 Nephi 11:16 may well refer to the fact that God the Father condescended to become the father of Jesus Christ,[6] it can also be taken to apply to God the Son. That is because the Book of Mormon teaches, as does the Gospel of John, that Jesus was divine and, under the Father's direction, created the earth. With this understanding, it is clear that the premortal Jesus Christ was in most instances the God interacting with his people in the Book of Mormon. In the same sense, he is understood to be the

Jehovah of the Old Testament. Accordingly, the divine Jehovah setting aside his premortal glory and power to become the helpless babe in swaddling clothes was an act of incomprehensible condescension. That act was also described by the Apostle Paul when he wrote that Jesus "made himself of no reputation, and took upon him the form of a servant, and was made in the likeness of men" (Philippians 2:7). This Book of Mormon teaching about the condescension makes the events of that first Christmas night all the more miraculous as we realize the scope and majesty of that Christ child in the manger and the full reason for his coming into the world.

As his vision continues, Nephi sees how this condescension will occur. The angel explains to Nephi that the virgin that he had seen is "the mother of the Son of God, after the manner of the flesh." After seeing the virgin caught away by the Spirit for a period of time, Nephi sees her return, still a virgin but carrying a child in her arms (1 Nephi 11:19–20).[7] This passage clarifies Isaiah 7:14, which refers to an *'almâ,* or "young woman," being found with child. It also supports Matthew's use of *parthenos,* or "virgin," when he translated this passage of Isaiah in his first formula quotation (Matthew 1:22–23; see Chapter 1: Son of

Wikimedia

Crucifixion, by Titian. Nephi saw the crucifixion of Jesus in a vision.

David). Nephi's vision thus confirms Gabriel's message to Mary at the Annunciation that she would be overshadowed by "the power of the Highest" and bear "the Son of God" (Luke 1:35).

Nephi's angel announces that this baby is "the Lamb of God, . . . even the Son of the Eternal Father" and then connects him with several important symbols, including "the tree of life" and a "fountain of living waters" (1 Nephi 11:21–25). Both of these symbols are equated with the love of God, which also represent Jesus, because "God so loved the world, that he gave his only begotten Son" (John 3:16).[8] The love of God is identified not only as being "most desirable above all things" but also as being "most joyous to the soul" (1 Nephi 11:22–23), connecting this message with so many other joyful Christmas stories. Situated as they are at the midpoint of Nephi's vision, these symbols of Christ serve as the interpretive centerpiece of the entire revelation. But the love of God is not only manifested in God sending his Son or in Jehovah condescending to become Jesus. With a second reference to the condescension of God, the angel then shows Jesus' earthly mission to Nephi, culminating in his mock trial, crucifixion, and death (1 Nephi 11:26–33). In a very direct way, then, Nephi's vision connects the miracle of Christmas to the even greater miracle of Easter.

KING BENJAMIN'S STORY

Another important passage from the Book of Mormon that affirms and deepens the biblical Christmas story comes from King Benjamin's sermon. Preparing to relinquish the kingdom to his son Mosiah, Benjamin gathers his people to give them final guidance and bear his last testimony. He begins by relating to his people the story of an angelic encounter that he experienced, in which an angel awakened him and began his message with these familiar words: "I am come to declare unto you the *glad tidings of great joy*" (Mosiah 3:3; emphasis added). The words of that angel thus anticipate the message that the angel of the Lord gives the shepherds on the night Christ was born, and the close parallel in the wording between "glad tidings of great joy" and "good tidings of great joy" is clearly significant.

In both cases, the initial joy in this message will arise because of the birth of the Son of God, but ultimately the joyful tidings are about the gospel itself, the "good news" of what the promised Savior will do for his people. The angel explains that he is giving this message to Benjamin so that the king could rejoice and then pass on the message to his people so "that they may also be filled with joy" (Mosiah 3:4), and the message that the angel delivers combines the joy of both Christmas and Easter. First, Benjamin and his people should rejoice because "the time cometh, and is not far distant, that with power, the Lord Omnipotent who reigneth, who was, and is from all eternity to all eternity, shall come down from heaven among the children of men, and shall dwell in a tabernacle of clay" (Mosiah 3:5). Once again, we see Book of

Christ Healing the Sick at Bethesda, *by Carl Bloch. The angel told King Benjamin that Jesus' ministry would include healing the sick.*

Hope Gallery

"And the Word Was Made Flesh"
John's Testimony and Abinadi's Sermon

Nephi's vision of the condescension and the incarnation of Jesus and Benjamin's story of the angel's message reveal a close correspondence between the portrayal of Jesus in the Book of Mormon and that reflected in the Gospel of John. Both have a very high Christology, that is, a very elevated and divine description of the person and work of the Christ. Unlike the Gospel of Mark—which demonstrates that Jesus is the Son of God primarily through a divine proclamation at his baptism, his miracles, and his authoritative ministry—or even Matthew and Luke, who attest his divinity through their stories of Jesus' divine conception and miraculous birth, John and the Book of Mormon both maintain that Jesus was the Christ from the beginning and that he was divine before his birth.[9]

John emphatically states this in the prologue to his Gospel: "In the beginning was the Word, and the Word was with God, *and the Word was God.* The same was in the beginning with God. All things were made by him; and without him was not any thing made that was made" (John 1:1–3; emphasis added). Describing the incarnation, John testifies, "*And the Word was made flesh,* and dwelt among us, (and we beheld his glory, the glory as of the only begotten of the Father,) full of grace and truth" (John 1:14; emphasis added).

A Book of Mormon parallel to this is found in Abinadi's words to the priests of King Noah: "I would that ye should understand that *God himself shall come down among the children of men,* and shall redeem his people. And *because he dwelleth in the flesh he shall be called the Son of God,* and having subjected the flesh to the will of the Father, being the Father and the Son—the Father, because he was conceived by the power of God; and *the Son, because of the flesh;* thus becoming the Father and Son" (Mosiah 15:1–3; emphasis added). Standard Latter-day Saint approaches to understanding this passage include discussing the absolute unity that exists between the Father and the Son; noting how Jesus functions as the "father of heaven and earth," or the Creator; stressing how he is the covenant father of those who abide in his gospel; and emphasizing the Son's role as the agent of the Father—whereby he speaks and acts through "divine investiture of authority."[10]

But if the title *Father* is equated with divinity and *Son* with mortality,[11] Abinadi is also agreeing with John that the Only Begotten of the Father was himself divine prior to the incarnation, condescending to mortality by subjecting his divine spirit to the flesh of his earthly tabernacle. As the Lord himself explained to Joseph Smith, "I am in the Father, and the Father in me, and the Father and I are one—the Father because he gave me of his fulness, and the Son because I was in the world and made flesh my tabernacle, and dwelt among the sons of men" (D&C 93:3–4).

Mormon prophecy deepening the meaning of the Christmas miracle. Jesus was not just the Son of David, the promised Savior, or even the Son of God—he was himself divine,[12] and his "dwelling in a tabernacle of clay" is the equivalent of John's description of the incarnation: "And the Word was made flesh, and dwelt among us" (John 1:14). A few verses later, Benjamin relates the exact identity of

Jesus, explaining that "he shall be called Jesus Christ, the Son of God, the Father of heaven and earth, the Creator of all things from the beginning; and his mother shall be called Mary" (Mosiah 3:8). As Joseph in Matthew's account—and Mary in Luke's—learned Jesus' name through angelic revelation, so here an angel makes the name known to King Benjamin many years earlier. Further, the revelation of Mary's role before its fulfillment, and indeed her very name, emphasizes her important mission in bringing forth the Son of God.

These references to Jesus' incarnation and his birth to Mary—focusing on *who* he would *be*—are interwoven with prophetic descriptions of *what* he would *do*. First, after describing how he would dwell in a tabernacle of clay, Benjamin explains to his people that the angel had told him how the Lord would "go forth amongst men, working mighty miracles, such as healing the sick, raising the dead, causing the lame to walk, the blind to receive their sight, and the deaf to hear, and curing all manner of diseases. And he shall cast out devils, or the evil spirits which dwell in the hearts of the children of men" (Mosiah 3:5–6). This healing and serving ministry is followed by a prophecy of his salvific suffering: "And lo, he shall suffer temptations, and pain of body, hunger, thirst, and fatigue, even more than man can suffer, except it be unto death; for behold, blood cometh from every pore, so great shall be his anguish for the wickedness and the abominations of his people" (Mosiah 3:7). Then, after the reference to the prophesied names of Jesus and Mary, the angel describes Jesus' rejection, abuse, crucifixion, and, finally, Resurrection. Indeed, Benjamin's story ties its prophecies of Jesus' coming more closely to his saving work than does either Matthew or Luke, and the interweaving of references to both his birth and his Atonement again inextricably link Christmas with Easter.

ALMA'S TESTIMONY

While preaching to the Nephite church at Gideon, Alma the Younger bears powerful testimony of the coming Savior. Inspired to preach to the people, Alma calls them to repentance and enjoins them to prepare the way of the Lord, anticipating many of the same words that would be spoken by Jesus' best known prophetic forerunner, John the Baptist. Alma is moved to preach this way because "the kingdom of heaven is at hand, and the Son of God cometh upon the face of the earth" (Alma 7:9). The testimony that follows is both a direct confirmation of vital truths from Matthew and Luke and a deep theological reflection on what Jesus would do.

Just as Benjamin had done earlier, Alma prophesies that the name of Jesus' mother will be Mary, again stressing that she will be "a precious and chosen vessel" (Alma 7:10). While Latter-day Saints do not venerate Mary as do some Christian traditions, Book of Mormon references to her and her mission, such as this one, make clear the honor and respect with which she should be regarded. As in Gabriel's annunciation to Mary, Alma explains that she will "be overshadowed" and bring forth a son who will be the Son of God (see Luke 1:35). Likewise, Alma's reference to her "conceiv[ing] by the power of the Holy Ghost" evokes the meaning of the Greek behind the phrase in Matthew 1:20:

"that which is conceived in her is *by* (Greek, *ek;* KJV, "of") the Holy Ghost" (see Chapter 1: Son of David). Finally, Alma prophesies the birth will take place not in Nazareth, Mary's home, but "at" or near Jerusalem, which implies Bethlehem, which is only five miles from the capital, being in the land of Jerusalem.[13]

While these prophetic details confirm elements of the biblical accounts, most of the focus of Alma's testimony is on *what* the promised Savior will accomplish. In one of the great Christological contributions of the Book of Mormon, Alma articulates the breadth of the Atonement of Jesus Christ. First, he clearly describes how Christ will overcome the two great obstacles, death and sin, that keep us from returning to and being like God: "And he will take upon him death, that he may loose the bands of death which bind his people" and "the Son of God suffereth according to the flesh that he might take upon him the sins of his people, that he might blot out their transgressions according to the power of his deliverance" (Alma 7:12, 13).

Second, around and between these passages Alma interweaves teachings about the power of Christ's Resurrection and redemption, which are profound proclamations about the healing power of the Atonement. Alma does this by expanding upon a principle taught earlier

Hope Gallery

The Annunciation, *by Carl Bloch. Alma testified that the mother of the Son of God would be named Mary.*

by Isaiah, who prophesied how God's chosen servant "hath borne our griefs, and carried our sorrows" (Isaiah 53:4). While this passage of Isaiah was quoted by Abinadi and was later paraphrased by Matthew as well (Mosiah 14:4; Matthew 8:17), Alma's testimony provides these additional, eloquent details: "And he shall go forth, suffering pains and afflictions and temptations of every kind; and this that the word might be fulfilled which saith he will take upon him the pains and the sicknesses of his people. And he will take upon him . . . their infirmities, that his bowels may be filled with mercy, according to the flesh,

Bearing Our Infirmities

It is difficult to look at any newborn baby and accept that he or she will necessarily encounter pain, challenges, disappointments, and hardships in life. Yet even the Savior needed to "go forth, suffering pains and afflictions . . . of every kind" (Alma 7:11), the only difference being that Jesus, though tempted, did not sin (Hebrews 4:15; see also D&C 45:4). Even harder to comprehend, however, was how that precious Babe of Bethlehem, whose birth we celebrate each Christmas, would one day bear the weight not only of our sins but also all our infirmities.

Infirmities are basically weaknesses, and like sins they make us unlike God, separating us from him and keeping us from returning to his presence and enjoying the kind of eternal life that he has. The ultimate physical weakness is death. Christ's triumph over that obstacle is what we celebrate each Easter. In addition, sickness, physical pain, and the difficulties of age—all forerunners of death—can and will be conquered by Christ as well, either through miracles and healings in this life or through the restoration that comes in the Resurrection.[14] But there are other infirmities, not always as visible, that afflict souls, hearts, and minds. Depression, discouragement, disappointment, and heartache, together with emotional and psychological ailments not so easily seen or connected to physical causes, can also be covered by the healing power of the Atonement.

As the author of Hebrews teaches, we do not have a great high priest who "cannot be touched with the feelings of our infirmities" (Hebrews 4:15). Instead, Alma testifies that Jesus has taken upon himself our infirmities that he may know how to succor (Latin, *succurro*, meaning "run to help or rescue") us, in *all* our needs.

that he may know according to the flesh how to succor his people according to their infirmities" (Alma 7:11, 12). Once again the Infancy is intertwined with the Passion and the Resurrection.

SAMUEL THE LAMANITE'S PROPHECY

Some five years before Jesus was born in Bethlehem, a prophet of Lamanite extraction named Samuel came to the city of Zarahemla to preach to the Nephites. After preaching repentance for many days, Samuel was expelled, only to be compelled by the Spirit to return and preach to the Nephites a second time. In his second set of sermons, Samuel prophesied that because of their hardness, destruction awaited the Nephites, a calamity that they could have avoided if they had heeded his earlier message of repentance (Helaman 13:2–6). But Samuel also tells his listeners that on his first mission he had been instructed to share "glad tidings," which had first been declared unto him by an angel (Helaman 13:7).

While the Nephites had missed the opportunity to hear these glad tidings the first time Samuel had preached to them, this important message about the coming birth of the Savior was nonetheless

included in his second set of decla-
rations to them. After preaching to
them at length about their wickedness and the destructions that were
coming, Samuel declares: "Behold
I give you a sign; for five years
more cometh, and behold, then
cometh the Son of God to redeem
all those who shall believe in his
name. And behold, this will I give
unto you for a sign at the time of
his coming; for behold, there shall
be great lights in heaven, insomuch that in the night before he
cometh there shall be no darkness,
insomuch that it shall appear unto
man as if it was day" (Helaman
14:2–3). Samuel explains that as
a result there would be a day, a
night, and a day as if there had
been no night, and continues,
"And behold, there shall a new star
arise, such an one as ye never have
beheld" (Helaman 14:5).

While the image of a new star
arising immediately resonates with

Mary and the Resurrected Lord, *by Harry Anderson. Samuel prophesied that Jesus Christ would bring about the resurrection of the dead.*

Matthew's story of a "star in the east" (with the Greek meaning "at its rising," see Chapter 4: King of Israel), Samuel's prophecy was about more than just the Nativity. Samuel explains that those who believe on the Son of God will have eternal life, whereas those who reject this glad message will fall under the judgments of God (Helaman 13:8–13). He pairs the signs of the Savior's birth with corresponding signs of his death (Helaman 14:14, 20–27). Thus the glad tidings of Jesus' birth are tempered by the solemn realization that his mission was not just to live but also to die, "For behold, he surely must die that salvation may come; yea, it behooveth him and becometh expedient that he dieth, to bring to pass the resurrection of the dead, that thereby men may be brought into the presence of the Lord. Yea, behold, this death bringeth to pass the resurrection, and redeemeth all mankind" (Helaman 14:15–16). Ultimately this is the real good news, the gospel—that through Jesus' suffering,

Jesus, the Light of the World

When Jesus was born, in the eastern hemisphere the Magi beheld a star and the shepherds saw angels, but in the western hemisphere *all* witnessed a night that was lit as brightly as the day, together with a new star. Among the Jews, darkness accompanied the Savior's final hours, and an earthquake and the tearing of the temple veil marked his death (Matthew 27:45, 51). For the children of Lehi, however, the destruction at the time of Jesus' death was cataclysmic; thick darkness lasted for three days (3 Nephi 8:5–23). Exactly why the signs in each instance were so much greater in the New World is not completely clear, but the stark contrast between a night without darkness and then days without light illustrate a fundamental truth from the Gospel of John, namely that Jesus is "the light of the world" (John 8:12).

While Jesus is in the world, there can be no lasting darkness, and when he is absent there can be no true light. In the world today, where there is knowledge of Christ even though he is not physically present, it is up to us, his disciples, to determine whether our lives are full of light or darkness. As the risen Lord told the Nephites, "hold up your light that it may shine unto the world. Behold *I am the light* which ye shall hold up" (3 Nephi 18:24; emphasis added).

The setting out of luminaria on Christmas Eve is a custom common among some New World Hispanics that our family adopted while living in New Mexico. One explanation is that the small bags with candles in them are meant to light the way for the Christ child.

Leroy Robertson, *Oratorio from the Book of Mormon*
Newell Dayley, "I Come unto My Own"

In 1938, LDS music educator Leroy Robertson (1896–1971) began a project that would occupy his mind and talents until 1953: the composition of an oratorio in the tradition of Handel that would be based upon the Book of Mormon. He had first conceived of the idea sometime about 1919 when he shared a train ride from Payson, Utah, to Pleasant Grove, Utah, with Elder Melvin J. Ballard, then a member of the Council of the Twelve, who suggested that he pursue such a project. Initially encouraged by the First Presidency to complete it for the 1947 centennial of the Mormon pioneers' arrival in Utah, he later completed it at the encouragement of Maurice Abravanel, conductor of the Utah Symphony, who directed its first performance in the Salt Lake Tabernacle on February 18, 1953.[15] Robertson's efforts were pivotal for LDS musical composition, encouraging or otherwise influencing subsequent works, including Robert Cundick's *The Song of Nephi* and *The Redeemer*; Newell Dayley's *Immanuel*; Crawford Gates's *Visions of Eternity*; and Merrill Jensen's *Come unto Christ*.[16]

Robertson's oratorio is divided into three parts: the first treats the prophecies of Samuel; the second, the signs of the Savior's birth; and the third, the destructions among the Nephites that led up to the appearance of the resurrected Christ. The second part provides a particularly moving testimony to the Book of Mormon's witness of Jesus' birth. After a dissonant chorus representing the unbelievers' taunt that the believers' joy and faith had been in vain (see 3 Nephi 1:6), Robertson set the Savior's words to Nephi in a movement that begins with a baritone soloist representing Jesus and then quickly divides into a full, four-part chorus. This part of the oratorio ends with an orchestral interlude titled "Pastorale." Adapted from Robertson's earlier *Deseret Symphony*, this movement follows the tradition of both Corelli and Handel's "Pastoral Symphony."[17]

A shorter but pleasing treatment of the Savior's words, "Lift up your head and be of good cheer; on this night shall the sign be given" (3 Nephi 1:13–14), is the choral arrangement "I Come unto My Own" by Latter-day Saint composer and musician K. Newell Dayley (1939–). A member of the Brigham Young University music faculty from 1967–2007, Dayley has composed a number of well-known LDS hymns and other musical selections. Written in 1978, this arrangement has been commercially published, most recently in 2006, making it available for LDS choirs and musical groups that wish to use a setting of a Book of Mormon passage for Christmas.[18]

death, and Resurrection we are saved from the effects of the Fall, of our individual sins and weaknesses, and of death itself.

After Samuel's departure from the land, some Nephites did repent, coming to Nephi, the son of Helaman, for baptism. This small but growing group of believers continued to have faith in the Lord's promised deliverance, just as Zacharias and Mary would. And just as Gabriel appeared to the two of them, and the angel of the Lord to the shepherds, among the Nephites also "angels did appear unto men, *wise men,* and did declare unto them glad tidings of great joy" (Helaman 16:14; emphasis added). These tidings no doubt witnessed both the beginning and the end of the greatest story that would ever be told—the coming birth, the necessary death, and the triumphant rising from death of the Savior of the world. Like the Nephite wise men and women and the later Magi, we too can wisely seek and joyfully receive this saving testimony of who Jesus Christ is and how he performed the Atonement for us.

NEPHI THE SON OF NEPHI'S STORY

Though some Nephites believed Samuel and Nephi, those believers of the good news soon found themselves threatened by unbelievers who conspired to kill all those who believed in the promised birth of the Savior and the signs that Samuel had prophesied would accompany it (3 Nephi 1:9). The prophet who confronted this threatened massacre was Nephi's son, also named Nephi. This Nephi despaired for his people, praying to the Lord for their deliverance over the course of an entire day. Finally, the voice of the Lord himself came to him: "Lift up your head and be of good cheer; for behold, the time is at hand, and on this night shall the sign be given, and on the morrow come I into the world" (3 Nephi 1:13).

This simple but powerful statement, directly from the one who would soon be the baby in the manger, no doubt filled Nephi with great joy. As prophesied, when the sun went down at the end of that day, no darkness followed, and along with the other signs, "a new star did appear, according to the word" (3 Nephi 1:15–21). Presumably this was the same star seen by the Magi in the Old World, but unlike there, where only those who were prepared and were looking for the sign seem to have seen it, among the Nephites the star and the other heavenly wonders were seen by all. For many, however, heavenly wonders were not enough to instill saving faith, and they again began to doubt and returned to wickedness, illustrating that only if we hold the Savior in our hearts do the glad tidings lead unto salvation. ❖

© Robert Barrett

The New Star, *by Robert Barrett.*

THE FOCUS OF ADVENT: SALVATION

Some Advent wreaths feature a white fifth candle, sometimes called the "Christ candle," that is placed in the middle of the wreath and is lit on Christmas Eve and Christmas Day. In our family, the lighting of this candle is the culmination of our Christmas Eve activities. After a special dinner and the production of our annual Nativity play, written by our children themselves and based as much on tradition and scripture videos as upon biblical texts, we light all five candles and have a more serious final Christmas reflection. After reading the words of Jesus in 3 Nephi 1:13–14, we then read the familiar Christmas story from Luke 2:1–14 and sing "Silent Night" together.

The fact that Advent also looks forward to Jesus' Second Coming can lead to our using this candle to think about the day when he will again be present with his people. But the great joy of both the Christmas and Easter messages is that Jesus Christ can always be present in our lives if we open our hearts to him. Indeed, in some traditions, this candle sometimes represents the Advent theme of Presence, meaning that the promised Messiah has at last arrived and is present with his people.[1]

On Christmas Eve we light all of the Advent candles, starting with the first purple candle and finishing with the central white candle.

However, given the emphasis of Book of Mormon Christmas passages on the salvation that Jesus' birth *and* death and Resurrection make possible, I have begun to consider this candle as representing a new fifth Advent theme, Salvation. In the biblical stories as well, the angel of the Lord told Joseph that he should call the baby "Jesus," or *Yēšûa'*, because "he shall save his people from their sins" (Matthew 1:21), and the canticles of Mary, Zacharias, and Simeon likewise included expressions of joy over the coming salvation (see Luke 1:69, 77; 2:30).

Because our family also uses Advent candles to symbolize covenants, lighting the white Christ candle on Christmas Eve symbolizes that the true Light has come into the world to usher in the new covenant prophesied by Jeremiah 31:31–34. The Lord himself referred to this covenant at the Last Supper when he said that the sacrament represented his "blood of the new testament [or "covenant"], which is shed for many" (Mark 14:24). He thus made possible the blessings and promises of the "new and everlasting covenant" mentioned throughout latter-day revelation, whereby we are promised all that God has if we have faith in Christ and make sacred covenants of our own in his name.

Some scriptures that might be worthwhile for reflection, if not for actual reading on Christmas Eve, include this passage in Jeremiah 31, and others that focus on the theme of salvation, such as the following:

"This is the day which the Lord hath made; we will rejoice and be glad in it. *Save now, I beseech thee* [Hebrew, *hosanna*], O Lord. . . . Thou art my God, and I will praise thee: thou art my God, I will exalt thee. O give thanks unto the Lord; for he is good: *for his mercy endureth for ever*" (Psalm 118:24–25, 28–29; emphasis added).

"And he said, It is a light thing that thou shouldest be my servant to raise up the tribes of Jacob, and to restore the preserved of Israel: I will also give thee for a light to the Gentiles, *that thou mayest be my salvation unto the end of the earth*" (Isaiah 49:6; emphasis added).

"And moreover, I say unto you, that *there shall be no other name given nor any other way nor means whereby salvation can come unto the children of men*, only in and through the name of Christ, the Lord Omnipotent" (Mosiah 3:17; emphasis added).

"That great and last sacrifice will be the Son of God, yea, infinite and eternal. *And thus he shall bring salvation to all those who shall believe on his name*; this being the intent of this last sacrifice, to bring about the bowels of mercy, which overpowereth justice, and bringeth about means unto men that they may have faith unto repentance" (Alma 34:14–15; emphasis added).

Each year Samuel and Rachel write and perform their own Nativity play on Christmas Eve, often including their parents and Nana.

A new and sweetly stirring tradition that Elaine and I added to our final Advent celebration in 2010 was to end it with the singing of the sacrament hymn "Jesus, Once of Humble Birth." Its words, by Apostle Parley P. Pratt (1807–1857), are set to a tune adapted from Giacomo Meyerbeer (1791–1864). As Karen Davidson observes in her study of Latter-day Saint hymns, "This hymn is a triumphant meditation on the paradoxes of the Savior's life and ministry. . . . On the one hand are the poverty, pain, and submissiveness of the Savior's life; on the other hand are his sovereignty and power, the miracles of his atonement and resurrection."[2] Singing it on Christmas Eve reminds us of what the Babe of Bethlehem did when he first came into the world, as well as what he will yet do when he comes again on earth to reign.

Jesus, once of humble birth,
Now in glory comes to earth.
Once he suffered grief and pain;
Now he comes on earth to reign.
Now he comes on earth to reign.

Once a meek and lowly Lamb,
Now the Lord, the great I Am.
Once upon the cross he bowed;
Now his chariot is the cloud.
Now his chariot is the cloud.

Once he groaned in blood and tears;
Now in glory he appears.
Once rejected by his own,
Now their King he shall be known.
Now their King he shall be known.

Once forsaken, left alone,
Now exalted to a throne.
Once all things he meekly bore,
But he now will bear no more.
But he now will bear no more.[3]

In marked contrast to this sobering hymn, no Christmas is complete without hearing or singing the joyful strains of Handel's great "Hallelujah Chorus." When we remember that *halleluyah* is Hebrew for "praise YHWH," or Jehovah, it is a wonderful way to thank the Lord for the salvation that he has brought us.

Conclusion
REMEMBERING CHRISTMAS

As we seek Christ, as we find Him, as we follow Him, we shall have the Christmas spirit,
not for one fleeting day each year, but as our constant companion always.

—President Thomas S. Monson[1]

If I am not careful, a certain melancholy is likely to settle over me late each Christmas afternoon. All the preparation for the season comes to a climax on Christmas Eve and Christmas morning. When the gifts are all opened, when the Christmas meal is at last finished, when the celebration is all over, the joy of Christmas is sometimes replaced by a certain sadness. When this occurs, it is clear to me that my studying, reading, singing, and devotions in advance of Christmas may not have been enough. My efforts to make Christmas a more spiritual occasion have not been successful if giving and receiving gifts, having fun, and eating are still the real focus of my season. As President Monson observed, if we want the Christmas spirit to last, we must seek Christ, find him, and then follow him. To have the spirit of the season with us always, we need to do more than celebrate Christmas; we need to remember what it means every day.

BEGINNING WITH CHRISTMAS DAY

We may need to begin our efforts to remember the Christmas spirit on Christmas Day itself. Our family prepares spiritually for Christmas throughout December. Those efforts culminate on Christmas Eve—we light luminaria, put on our Nativity play, read from Luke 2, sing, share testimonies, and pray together. Clearly, Christ is the center of our celebration that evening, but if we do not make an effort, our focus on him can be lost the next morning.

This was apparent to me one year when extended family celebrated the holiday with us. We enjoyed having them around, but I became distracted by the commotion that accompanied many other people, some not familiar with our traditions. On Christmas morning, feeling some loss, I asked if we could pause before we opened our gifts and join in family prayer. That has become a new tradition: after gathering in the magical semidarkness of a living room lit only by Christmas lights and candles, we kneel and thank God for the great gift of his Son, and thank him for the bounty that allows us to give and receive the gifts that we will share. Only then do we descend into the family room to see what Santa has brought the children, returning later to open our gifts to each other by the Christmas tree.

Sermon on the Mount, by Carl Bloch.
Courtesy Hope Gallery.

135

Our new tradition is a small thing perhaps, but remembering Jesus first on Christmas morning has brought the glad tidings back into our celebration. That morning prayer, together with the more traditional Christmas dinner prayer, gives us an opportunity to thank God both for the good tidings of Jesus' birth and the glad tidings of his love and sacrifice represented by the Atonement and Resurrection that we celebrate at Easter. Beyond these efforts with my family, I find that I must take time that day to think about the meaning of God's gift of his Son. Just as I try to study, reflect, and worship in the weeks leading up to Christmas, I am blessed when, even in the excitement of Christmas Day, I take time for what George Durrant calls *true* Christmas time"—sacred time to slow down, reflect, remember, pray, and feel the spirit of this wonderful holiday.[2]

THE BOY IN THE TEMPLE AND THE MAN OF THE GOSPELS

Traditionally, Christmas was a season, not a single day. Rather than being a countdown to the big day, the Twelve Days were a celebration that began with Christmas and stretched to Epiphany on January 6. Lately our family has tried to recapture that sense of a *season* of celebration rather than just a day. While we still take down our tree and many of our decorations on New Year's Day, we have started leaving our outside Christmas lights on until January 5, the night our family reads the story of the Wise Men from Matthew 2. And rather than ending our December pattern of reading and singing together each evening, we read some of the other stories that follow the birth and the adoration of the shepherds, such as the Presentation in the Temple and then the story of Jesus as a boy, teaching in that same temple (Luke 2:41–52).

Luke's brief but well-known account, the only canonical "boyhood story" in the scriptures, serves as a link between Luke's Infancy Narrative and the rest of his Gospel. Joseph and Mary, returning to Nazareth, panic when they realize that Jesus is not among their company. They find him at last in the temple. When they asked Jesus why he had dealt with them so, his response added his own witness of his identity and mission to the testimonies borne by angels, shepherds, Simeon, Anna, and the Wise Men: "How is it that ye sought me? wist ye not that I must be about my Father's business?" (Luke 2:49). We do not know exactly when the veil of forgetfulness that falls upon us all began to thin for the Son of God. We know that he did not receive of the fulness at first, receiving instead grace for grace (see D&C 93:12–14), but at twelve he already possessed great knowledge and wisdom, being able to converse with the sages in the temple, both asking them questions and giving them answers that astonished them (JST, Luke 2:46–47). Above all, he knew who he was—the Son of the Father—and that he had come to do his Father's work.

Luke's story concludes with Jesus returning to Nazareth with his parents, being subject to them as he "increased in wisdom and stature, and in favour with God and man" (Luke 2:51–52). This bridge between the Infancy Narratives and later accounts of Jesus' adult ministry is echoed in Joseph Smith's translation of the end of Matthew's account of Jesus' childhood, which adds a scene not in the King

James Version: "And it came to pass that Jesus grew up with his brethren, and waxed strong, and waited upon the Lord for the time of his ministry to come. And he served under his father, and he spake not as other men, neither could he be taught; for he needed not that any man should teach him" (JST, Matthew 3:24–26).

Reading and studying the stories of the Savior's birth prepares us to celebrate the gift of the Babe of Bethlehem, helping us to know who this promised Savior was. If we follow our Christmas celebrations with the story of the Boy in the Temple and then continue to read about our Lord and Savior Jesus Christ after the holiday is over, then we will come to know and celebrate the Man of the Gospels throughout the year, preparing us to learn from him and understand truly what he was born to do. In 1983, President Gordon B. Hinckley emphasized the importance of reading and studying the Gospels and the Book of Mormon in order to better know the Savior: "Let us establish in our lives the habit of reading those things which will strengthen our faith in the Lord Jesus Christ, the Savior of the world. He is the pivotal figure of our theology and our faith. Every Latter-day Saint has the responsibility to know for himself or herself with a certainty beyond doubt that Jesus is the resurrected, living Son of the living God."[3] President Hinckley then went on to recommend a program of reading "a chapter a day of the Gospels—that is, Matthew, Mark, Luke, and John in the Bible; and Third Nephi in the Book of Mormon, particularly beginning with the eleventh chapter of Third Nephi where is found the account of Christ's visit among the Nephites."[4]

GLAD TIDINGS EVERY DAY

Continuing to study the scriptural testimonies of Jesus Christ can take the good tidings of the Savior's birth and turn them into the daily glad tidings of a living, saving faith that will change both us and those around us. Speaking of this, President Thomas S. Monson has taught, "Born in a stable, cradled in a manger, He came forth from heaven to live on earth as mortal man and to establish the kingdom of God. During his earthly ministry, He taught men the higher law. His glorious gospel reshaped the thinking of the world. He blessed the sick. He caused the lame to walk, the blind to see, the deaf to hear. He even raised the dead to life. To us, He has said, 'Come, follow me.'"[5] As we strive to follow the Savior, we can extend the spirit of love and giving that abounds so much at Christmastime and enjoy it every day as we strive to love and serve those whom he loves. Helping the needy, visiting the sick and lonely, and sharing time with loved ones brings joy into the Christmas season to be sure, but doing these things throughout the year truly blesses others and makes us more like Jesus Christ.

When we learn about the Man of the Gospels and then follow his example, we are led ultimately to the Savior, who gave himself that we might live. As the Book of Mormon clearly teaches, tidings of the Savior's birth are integrally connected to the good news of what he accomplished in the final days of his life. Thus, as we move in our hearts and minds from Christmas to Easter, each day can be filled with glad tidings of great joy as we celebrate the teachings, miracles, and mission of Jesus, culminating in his terrible suffering, his saving death, and his glorious Resurrection. ❖❖

Appendix 1

THE INFANCY NARRATIVES AND THE CHRISTMAS STORY

Of all the biblical sources, only Matthew and Luke provide narratives—or stories—of the conception, birth, and early years of Jesus. In Paul's writings, often accepted as among the earliest documents found in the New Testament, only two references, Galatians 4:4 and Romans 1:3, make any reference to the birth or ancestry of Jesus. More striking is the lack of Infancy Narratives in Mark and John's Gospels. To understand the Infancy Narratives in context, it is important to consider the issue of Gospel beginnings, particularly how each Gospel is influenced by its author's emphasis on differing aspects of Jesus' person and work. Also helpful is a consideration of how the Infancy Narratives function as parts of the larger Gospels of Matthew and Luke.

GOSPEL BEGINNINGS AND CHRISTOLOGY

Even before there was a written Gospel, the gospel, or "good news" (Greek, *euangellion*) about Jesus was found in apostolic preaching about Jesus. Known as the *kērygma,* from the Greek for "proclamation," this preaching focused on a basic message about Jesus: God had sent his Son, who suffered and died for mankind, was raised from the dead, and ascended into heaven, from whence he would return to judge the earth and save his Saints. This is the message of Peter's earliest speeches as preserved in the book of Acts and most of Paul's letters. For the early Christians, the emphasis of the *kērygma* was on what Christ had done for them. The heart of apostolic preaching was the message of the salvific Atonement and Resurrection of Jesus. As a result, when preaching, Paul was determined to teach nothing "save Jesus Christ, and him crucified" (1 Corinthians 2:2). The clearest sign that Jesus was the Son of God was that he had been "declared [Greek, *oristhentos,* "designated, marked, or appointed"] to be the Son of God with power, according to the spirit of holiness, by the resurrection from the dead" (Romans 1:4).

Assumed to be the first-written of the Gospels, Mark followed the basic pattern of apostolic preaching in its structure and development. Peter's preaching has been considered the basis for the Gospel of Mark.[1] Interestingly, Mark follows an expanded version of the *kērygma* that appears in Peter's speech to Cornelius: "God anointed Jesus of Nazareth with the Holy Ghost and with power: *who went about doing good, and healing all that were oppressed of the devil;* for God was with him. And we are witnesses of all things which he did . . . ; whom they slew and hanged upon a tree: Him God raised up on the third day, and shewed him openly" (Acts 10:38–40; emphasis added). The detail that Jesus went about doing good and healing those who were captive to the devil is echoed in Mark's account of Jesus' ministry (Mark 1–13).

Nevertheless, the focus of Mark's Gospel remained his Passion and Resurrection Narratives (Mark 14–16), with their story of the suffering and rising of Jesus reflecting the central theme of the early Christian *kērygma.* Indeed, this is the focus of all four canonical Gospels, and because this is the one series of events where John's narrative roughly accords with the other three Gospels, some have suggested that all four authors were following a primitive Passion Narrative, either oral, as in the *kērygma* preaching tradition, or perhaps written.[2] This is because the Atonement and

Resurrection of Jesus form the heart of his saving work—what he came to the world to *do* (see John 3:16–17). In biblical scholarship, this is one of the two major parts of the study of Christology: the examination of the *person* and the *work* of Jesus Christ. All the Gospels answer the second part of the Christological question by ending with accounts of Jesus' Passion and Resurrection. Likewise, they each begin by setting forth who Jesus *was* as the Messiah, but they begin at different points. Some scholars have proposed that this reflects an evolution in early Christian understanding about what it meant that Jesus was the Son of God,[3] but the authors could have been emphasizing different aspects of his identity, with later authors clarifying points that had been missed by the earlier accounts.

Mark's Gospel begins at the outset of Jesus' ministry, with John the Baptist's mission and an account of Jesus' baptism. While Paul in Romans 1:4 suggested that the greatest proof of Jesus' divine Sonship was found in his Resurrection, Mark's proof that Jesus was the Christ was God declaring that Jesus is his Son: "And straightway coming up out of the water, he saw the heavens opened, and the spirit like a dove descending upon him; And there came a voice from heaven saying, *Thou art my beloved Son,* in whom I am well pleased" (Mark 1:10–11; emphasis added). Jesus was the Son of God because God had declared it, though implicitly the descent of the Spirit upon Jesus also fulfilled Peter's words that "God anointed Jesus of Nazareth with the Holy Ghost *and with power*" (Acts 10:38; emphasis added). Indeed, in Mark's narrative, another sign that Jesus is the Son of God is his authoritative ministry, in which he heals and acts with power.

While Mark's proofs of Jesus' identity are correct, taken alone they are certainly incomplete. Just as some could misinterpret Paul's Resurrection Christology to mean that Jesus was not truly the Son of God until he was raised from the dead in glory, one could adopt from Mark what some scholars have termed an Adoptionist Christology. That is, Jesus was only the Son of God because God adopted him at baptism, proclaiming him his Son and pouring his Spirit and power upon him. Within a decade of Mark's writing, scholars believe, Matthew and then Luke felt impressed to clarify that Jesus was *actually* God's Son, conceived and born as such in what has been termed a Conception Christology. Their efforts also responded to what was growing interest among early Christians about Jesus' background and birth. With the addition of Infancy Narratives at the beginning of their Gospels, Matthew and Luke carefully composed their Gospels. Beginning with well-crafted accounts of *who* Jesus was, they balanced their stories with Passion and Resurrection Narratives that explained *what* he had done.

John, thought to be, not unanimously, the last-written of the Gospels, advances Christological teaching further by starting "in the beginning" and emphasizing that Jesus was not just the Son of God but was divine himself (see John 1:1–5). This Premortal Christology takes the place of what might have been an Infancy Narrative. John nonetheless teaches the divine conception and miraculous birth of Jesus by stating: "And the word was made flesh" (John 1:14). While Mary is never named in John, she is an important figure at the beginning of his ministry at the wedding at Cana (John 2:1–11) and then again at the Crucifixion (John 19:25–27). I have suggested elsewhere that the miracle of water changed into wine may be a symbol of the Incarnation, as the Divine Word becomes the mortal Jesus.[4] If so, Mary's presence at the wedding would symbolize her role as Jesus' mother, making her at the beginning of John's Gospel a witness of whom Jesus is and again, at the end, of what he had come to do.

THE INFANCY NARRATIVES AND THE GOSPELS OF MATTHEW AND LUKE

The narratives that Matthew and Luke composed to begin their Gospels constitute a distinct genre of writing. The two accounts share much with each other and gave rise to some later apocryphal imitations in the early centuries of Christianity. Though common in scholarship, the term *Infancy Narrative* is not exact, because most of Matthew 1 and all of Luke 1 describe events *before* Jesus' birth, and Luke 2:41–52 relates a story from Jesus' boyhood. They are sometimes called *Infancy Gospels,* though in many ways this term fits better for stand-alone postbiblical works that elaborated on the story of Jesus' nativity and boyhood as well as Mary's background. Some of these apocryphal works include the Protoevangelium (literally, "before the gospel") of James, the Infancy Gospel of Thomas, the Arabic Infancy Gospel, and the Gospel of Pseudo-Matthew. Dating from the mid–second century to as late as the sixth, these extracanonical works cannot be relied upon for either historical or theological details about Jesus.[5]

Certain factors suggest that the Infancy Narratives, though they appear first in the Gospels and serve as their introductions, were, in fact, written last. First, both Matthew and Luke could begin in their respective third chapters, with an account of John the Baptist's ministry and his baptism of Jesus, as Mark's Gospel does. Second, none of the details provided in the Infancy Narratives are referred—or even alluded—to later in their respective Gospels. If the first two chapters of each of these Gospels had been lost at an early stage of their transmission, later readers would probably not notice their absence. On the other hand, each of the Infancy Narratives supports the themes and imagery that characterize the rest of their respective Gospel, raising the possibility that Matthew and Luke had each conceived their particular Gospel—and perhaps even drafted it—before feeling the need to compose a narrative that would treat the important question of who Jesus was and how he was born.[6]

Possibly appended later to their Gospels, the Infancy Narratives are compositions that could nonetheless stand alone as self-contained stories. A mix of third-person narration of events, quoted discourse, and dramatic episodes, both of them consist of a series of stories that are carefully interwoven to both introduce how and why Jesus is the Son of God as well as establish patterns and symbols that support the larger Gospels. This has led one set of commentators to describe them as "overtures" that, like musical overtures, provide a foretaste of the motifs, themes, and movement of the larger work.[7] Thus, Matthew's establishment in his Gospel of Jesus as "the Son of David" in his Infancy Narrative lays the groundwork for his depiction of Jesus as the Jewish Messiah later. Likewise, the image of Christ as a new Moses, as depicted in Matthew's accounts of the Herodian attempt to slay him and his return from Egypt, anticipates Jesus' role as the new lawgiver in the Sermon on the Mount. Further, the division of Matthew's Gospel into five parts, hearkening back to the five books of Moses, is anticipated by five sets of dreams and five formula quotations in the Infancy Narrative.[8]

The Christology of Luke's Infancy Narrative, which emphasizes Jesus' role as the Son of God and the Savior for *all* people, accords with his subsequent portrayal of Jesus, where he is less exclusively a Jewish Messiah than in Matthew. The prominence of Elisabeth, Mary, and Anna in Luke's Infancy Narrative establishes precedent for his almost unique emphasis on women's role in Jesus' story, who appear with much more frequency in Luke than they do in any of the other Gospels. Another emphasis in Luke is concern for the poor and the marginalized, who are highlighted both in the *Magnificat* and in the shepherds' appearance at the manger rather than the wise, rich, and powerful. Likewise, the centrality of the Holy Spirit in John the Baptist's and Jesus' conceptions, as well as his role in inspiring Elisabeth, Zacharias, and Simeon, is an anticipation of the central role of the Spirit in Luke's Gospel and the book of Acts.[9] But above all, by emphasizing that Jesus is the Son of God, born to be the Savior, Luke's Infancy Narrative is, like Matthew's, "the essential Gospel story in miniature."[10]

The difference in theological focus and theme between these two Gospels partly accounts for their significant differences, though it is apparent that Matthew and Luke also had different sources for their stories. While Luke either shared some of the same sources as Matthew for the main part of his Gospel—or, perhaps, had access to Matthew's account—for his Infancy Narrative, Luke followed a different set of traditions and had somewhat different aims. By treating major divisions of each Infancy Narrative in separate chapters and by generally avoiding any attempt to harmonize the two accounts, I have tried in this book to emphasize the uniqueness of each account.

Matthew's Infancy Narrative is considerably more concise, about half the length of Luke's. If one excerpts Matthew's genealogy, Luke's account is almost four times as long. Matthew's account gives a central role to Joseph, who, as a son of David himself, provides the legal connection to the royal inheritance. But perhaps more importantly, Joseph appears in Matthew's account as a righteous Israelite, one who is just (or in harmony with law), considerate to his espoused wife, and protective of her and her child. A faithful man in the mode of Joseph in Egypt, who allows himself to be guided by revelation, he both served as the called foster father of Jesus and as a model for fathers—and even mothers—in every age. Jesus himself is presented as the rightful king, set against wicked kings such as Herod and his son Archelaus whose power is shown to be temporal and fleeting. In every scene, Jesus is seen as the fulfillment of prophecy, demonstrating how he came into the world, who he was, and where the important first events of his life took place.[11]

Luke's longer account includes several dramatic scenes as a prelude to his later description of the Nativity. Overall, Luke's narrative gives more background than Matthew's does, and it includes careful comparisons and contrasts that are best seen in the developed characters—such as Zacharias and Mary—that serve as foils to one another. Luke's focus on Mary is striking, leading some to suggest that she, or a member of her family, might have been one of Luke's sources. However, Luke's emphasis on Mary, and his relative exclusion of Joseph as an active character, emphasizes that Jesus is not in fact Joseph's son. Luke's poetic use of canticles both echo Old Testament salvation themes and make his stories deeply personal. By consciously imitating the style of the Septuagint and through highlighting the parallels between his subjects and Old Testament figures, Luke successfully connects the story of Jesus with the story of Israel, while at the time setting it on a wider world stage and broadening Jesus' role to all people. Above all, Luke emphasizes joy—the good news that the Savior of the world has been born.[12]

Still, substantive differences in the two accounts—particularly that Luke seems unaware of the Wise Men, the malevolent actions of Herod, or the flight to Egypt—continue to lead some to doubt the historicity of these stories. Nevertheless, on all the most important points, the two stories agree: Jesus' birth was long-prophesied, his mother was named Mary, and he was conceived in a miraculous and divine way, born in the city of David, and recognized by those who were led to him by revelation. These are the very points confirmed by Book of Mormon prophecy. ❖

Appendix 2

PREPARING FOR CHRISTMAS
A Family Resource Guide

In 1998, our family began the practice of taking time each day from December first to December twenty-fourth for a short Christmas devotional. The previous year, one of my aunts had given us a small booklet for Christmas that provided a scripture, a carol, and a Christmas story for each day leading up to Christmas. In addition to our weekly observance of Advent, this practice of holding a daily devotional has become a tradition for us. Each evening we gather in the living room, light the candles of our Advent wreath, and then read a story together, recite a scripture passage, and sing a carol before we join in family prayer. Our children have taken to calling this routine "doing Christmas," which is fitting, because our tradition has helped us focus on the true meaning of Christmas during the entire month.

Over the years we have developed and altered our Christmas Season Book, keeping it in a three-ring binder so that we can change it from time to time. My first change was to make a new selection of scriptures, drawing from the Latter-day Saint standard works and arranging them in rough chronological order to show how God revealed the good news of the coming of his Son, beginning with Adam and culminating with the annunciations to Mary and Joseph. In this appendix, I have provided the reference for each day's reading. These scriptural readings form the heart of each day's devotional.

Sometimes the carol suggestions match the scripture readings for the day, such as matching "Lo, How a Rose E'er Blooming" with the reading of the account of the annunciation to Mary on December 20. We enjoy singing a wide variety of Christmas songs, including a few from the *Children's Songbook*. Many carols can be found in the LDS hymnbook, but a few of the less common ones can be found in collections such as *The Christmas Songbook Treasury, 100 Carols for Choirs,* or *The New Oxford Book of Carols.*

Ideas of what makes a good story vary widely, and we continue to change our own ideas from year to year. For this resource guide, I have only included the titles of some of our current favorites, sometimes with a brief notation. The texts of most of these can be found on the Internet or in published collections. Families may want to make their own lists of stories based on their own preferences or on what they have readily available.

Although we usually end our devotionals with our Christmas Eve celebration, I have suggested additional selections that can be read after Christmas to help connect the Christmas season with the Gospels and Easter.

DECEMBER 1
Suggested story: O. Henry, "The Gift of the Magi." This well-known story of a poor young couple's love for each other is a nice way to begin the season as we start thinking of getting or making our own gifts for each other. We frequently shorten or summarize it for our children.
Suggested scripture: Moses 6:51–52, 57.
Suggested carol: "Angels We Have Heard on High," *Hymns,* no. 203.

DECEMBER 2

Suggested story: "On the Symbolism of Christmas," from "The Sixth Word," by Sherry Dillehay, *Especially for Mormons, Vol. 2.* This, or a story like it, can serve as a good vehicle for helping children understand the symbolism of so many of our Christmas decorations.

Suggested scriptures: Moses 1:6, 33, 39; Deuteronomy 18:15.

Suggested carol: "O Come, All Ye Faithful," *Hymns,* no. 202.

DECEMBER 3

Suggested story: "A Different Kind of Christmas," by Lael J. Littke. This touching story is set in pioneer-era Utah and describes the love that a mother who has lost her daughters develops for her foster son.

Suggested scriptures: 2 Samuel 7:12–14; Psalm 89:3–4, 28–29, 36–37.

Suggested carol: "Once in Royal David's City," *Hymns,* no. 205.

DECEMBER 4

Suggested story: "The Cobbler and His Guest," by Anne M. Boyles.

Suggested scripture: Psalm 24:9–10.

Suggested carol: "While Shepherds Watched Their Flocks," *Hymns,* no. 211.

DECEMBER 5

Suggested story: "It Takes a Child" (unknown author). In this story a homeless man teaches a mother about unconditional love.

Suggested scriptures: Isaiah 7:14; Matthew 1:23.

Suggested carol: "The First Noel," *Hymns,* no. 213.

DECEMBER 6

Suggested story: "Christmas Day in the Morning," by Pearl S. Buck. Later in life, a man reflects about the first, true Christmas gift he ever gave.

Suggested scripture: Isaiah 9:6–7.

Suggested carol: "Joy to the World," *Hymns,* no. 201.

DECEMBER 7

Suggested story: "In the Great Walled Country," by Raymond MacDonald Alden. A story mostly fit for young children.

Suggested scripture: Isaiah 11:1–4.

Suggested carol: "It Came upon a Midnight Clear," *Hymns,* no. 207.

DECEMBER 8

Suggested story: "A Brother Like That" (unknown author).

Suggested scripture: Isaiah 40:1–5.

Suggested carol: "Hark! The Herald Angels Sing," *Hymns,* no. 209.

DECEMBER 9

Suggested story: "Mr. Jinks Hands Out the Holly," *The Children's Friend,* December 1958.

Suggested scripture: Micah 5:2.

Suggested carol: "O Little Town of Bethlehem," *Hymns,* no. 208.

DECEMBER 10

Suggested story: "Keeping Baby Warm," by Lynda H. Laughlin.

Suggested scriptures: Jeremiah 23:5–6; see also 33:14–15.

Suggested carol: "Far, Far Away on Judea's Plains," *Hymns,* no. 212. This carol was written by Latter-day Saint composer John Menzies MacFarlane (1833–1892).

DECEMBER 11

Suggested story: "The Christmas Gift," by Hugh Oliver

Suggested scripture: 1 Nephi 10:4–5.

Suggested carol: "God Rest You Merry, Gentlemen," *100 Carols for Choirs,* no. 19.

DECEMBER 12

Suggested story: "The C-C-Choir Boy," by Fred Bauer. A boy with a stutter finds he can sing a solo in his school pageant if he only keeps his thoughts on the baby Jesus.

Suggested scripture: 1 Nephi 11:13–21.

Suggested carol: "What Child Is This?" *The New Oxford Book of Carols,* no. 98.

DECEMBER 13

Suggested story: "Bethann's Christmas Prayer," by Marilyn Morgan Helleberg. A young girl melts the heart of a sad, older woman who has suffered a terrible loss.

Suggested scripture: 2 Nephi 25:19, 26.

Suggested carol: "O Holy Night," *The Christmas Songbook Treasury,* 68.

DECEMBER 14

Suggested story: "Pattern of Love," by Jack Smith.

Suggested scripture: Jacob 4:4–5.

Suggested carol: "Bring a Torch, Jeanette, Isabella," *The Christmas Songbook Treasury,* 59.

DECEMBER 15

Suggested story: "The Littlest Angel," by Charles Tazewell. Though rather inaccurate doctrinally, this story makes a nice point about God's love for a child and his acceptance of gifts of the heart.

Suggested scripture: Jacob 7:11–12.

Suggested carol: "Go Tell It on the Mountain," *The New Oxford Book of Carols,* no. 169.

DECEMBER 16

Suggested story: "Special Delivery," by Mrs. Charles Stephan.

Suggested scripture: Malachi 3:1.

Suggested carol: "I Heard the Bells on Christmas Day," *Hymns,* no. 214.

DECEMBER 17

Suggested story: "The Little Match Girl," by Hans Christian Andersen.

Suggested scripture: Mosiah 3:5–8.

Suggested carol: "Picture a Christmas," *Children's Songbook,* 50.

DECEMBER 18

Suggested story: "Trouble at the Inn," by Dina Donahue. Another one of my favorites, this touching story is about a mentally slow boy whose tenderness causes a rather surprising change in the community Christmas pageant.

Suggested scripture: Alma 7:9–10.

Suggested carol: "Oh, Hush Thee, My Baby," *Children's Songbook,* 48.

DECEMBER 19

Suggested story: "I Knew You Would Come," by Elizabeth King English.

Suggested scripture: Helaman 14:2–8.

Suggested carol: "Stars Were Gleaming," *Children's Songbook,* 37.

DECEMBER 20

Suggested story: "Someone Missing at the Manger," by Elizabeth Starr Hill.

Suggested scripture: Luke 1:26–38.

Suggested carol: "Lo, How a Rose E'er Blooming," *100 Carols for Choirs,* no. 50.

DECEMBER 21

Suggested story: "Once in a Lifetime Christmas," by Will Wright. Without a doubt, this is one of my favorite stories that we read at Christmastime, recalling a Depression-era Christmas when an entire town worked together to give its children a Christmas they would always remember.

Suggested scripture: Matthew 1:18–25.

Suggested carol: "When Joseph Went to Bethlehem," *Children's Songbook,* 38.

DECEMBER 22

Suggested story: "The Gift of Love," by Thomas S. Monson.

Suggested scripture: Luke 1:39–56.

Suggested carol: "Away in a Manger," *Hymns,* no. 206.

DECEMBER 23

Suggested story: "Unexpected Christmas," by Marguerite Nixon. Another one of my favorites, this story tells of
a city couple who learn the true meaning of Christmas when they are forced to spend Christmas Eve with
a humble farming family.

Suggested scripture: 3 Nephi 1:13–14.

Suggested carol: "Once within a Lowly Stable," *Children's Songbook,* 41.

DECEMBER 24

Suggested scriptures: Luke 2:1–7; Matthew 1:25; Luke 2:8–16.

Suggested carol: "Silent Night," *Hymns,* no. 204.

CHRISTMAS DAY

Although we do not usually hold a devotional on Christmas Day, a personal tradition of mine is to read
or listen to George Durrant's retelling of his missionary Christmas. Alone, sick, and away from family, young
Elder Durrant spent the day with the biblical Christmas story, gaining his own testimony that Jesus Christ
was the Son of God (Durrant, "Don't Forget the Star," 30–38).

THE SUNDAY AFTER CHRISTMAS

Suggested scripture: Luke 2:21–39.

JANUARY 5 OR 6

Suggested story: "The Other Wise Man," by Henry Van Dyke.

Suggested scripture: Matthew 2:1–12.

Suggested carols: "With Wondering Awe," *Hymns,* no. 210, and "We Three Kings of Orient Are," *The Christmas
Songbook Treasury,* 46.

AFTER THE CHRISTMAS SEASON

Read the scriptures describing the flight to Egypt and return to Nazareth (Matthew 2:12–23) and of
the boy Jesus in the temple (Luke 2:41–52). After that, read one of the Gospels, or all of them, between
Christmas and Easter. Perhaps beginning on Palm Sunday, read the accounts of the final days of the Savior's
life, in preparation for celebrating the glad tidings of the Easter season.[1] ❖

Christ and the Young Child, *by Carl Bloch.* © *Intellectual Reserve, Inc.* "But Jesus said, Suffer little children, and forbid them not, to come unto me: for of such is the kingdom of heaven." *–Matthew 19:14*

Appendix 3

CHRISTMAS WITH AUTISM

Much of this book presupposes rather typical Christmases, where individuals or families can celebrate this most joyful of holidays with accustomed traditions and activities. For families with members who have special needs, however, this is not always the case. While this can make holidays difficult, it can also lead to new traditions and help all family members focus on the true meaning of Christmas. This became the case with my own family when, in April of 2008, our son, Samuel, was diagnosed with autism.

Samuel was four years old at the time, so by that point it was not a surprise. We had already noticed some differences, but at three and a half, he began to regress noticeably: his already slow language development halted, he stopped smiling, and, disturbingly, he no longer liked to be held and pushed us away whenever we tried to hold or hug him. The previous year he had been assessed as having a developmental delay as well as Sensory Processing Disorder (SPD). Nevertheless, the official autism diagnosis came with a certain finality that was devastating.

Autism is one of several developmental disorders known as Autism Spectrum Disorder (ASD). This is because features of ASD vary from child to child. As a result, our experiences with our son are not necessarily all that families who deal with autism encounter. We soon found that Samuel was only moderately affected, and he is now very high-functioning indeed. Part of this has been the result of prayer, faith, and blessings, but much has been due to hard work. After initial weeks of grief and some denial, we moved from management mode to proactive effort, doing everything we could to get him the early intervention that can often help ameliorate the impact of ASD. We had already enrolled him in a special education preschool, started him with private occupational therapy, and had begun some in-home therapy. Elaine became a tireless advocate for our son, taking on insurance companies and working actively with schools and therapists. I have always been a hands-on dad, but since then, working with family, teachers, a host of helpers, and the Lord, we have seen miracles with our boy.

Samuel is still somewhat verbally challenged, particularly in expressive language, but he has gone from very little language to being almost at age-level. He is still socially inhibited, but is incredibly warm and affectionate with our family and with a slightly larger circle of familiar people. To our joy, he now smiles infectiously and laughs easily. He now wants to be with and be like other children. Still, changes in routine and patterns are very disturbing to him, and his lingering SPD issues make lights, different tastes and smells, and loud noises such as singing in the ward Christmas program (or even weekly family home evenings) upsetting to him. This was difficult because I love to sing more than almost anything. Almost every time I began to sing, Samuel would scream or cover his ears.

These factors combined to make his third and fourth Christmases almost complete disasters, for reasons that we did not fully understand at the time. He wanted nothing to do with our daily Christmas devotionals and certainly did not want to be around for any of the singing. Different foods and smells at holiday time were not the source of fond associations for him as they were for the rest of us. Instead, they caused anxiety. Our traditional Christmas Eve picnic by the tree was such a nightmare that when he was three we ended up putting him in a playpen nearby simply to keep him from running away or wreaking havoc. Still, he cried the entire time, largely spoiling the evening, and including him in our Nativity play was not really an option. Christmas morning was, not surprisingly, a sensory overload, but when he focused on a single toy, he seemed to enjoy himself. Two Christmases ago he played single-mindedly all day long, ignoring almost everyone and everything else until he dropped into bed later that night. Nevertheless, as important as Christmas traditions are to me, I was gripped by an increasing feeling of sadness. Not only was Samuel not learning what we wanted him to learn about the season—let alone enjoying it fully—but his struggles were also affecting how the rest of us experienced the holiday. Our dreams of a bright future for our son had faded.

We have learned much about autism since his diagnosis. Even more, we have learned much about *Samuel*. Routines and patterns are important to him, but he can handle change if given the right preparation. He is a very visual learner, and he began to read at an early age. As a result, one of our specialists helped Elaine come up with the idea of using checklists when we mainstreamed him into kindergarten. Additionally, we purchased a magnetic whiteboard and divided it into columns for days and rows for mornings, afternoons, and evenings. Signs with both pictures and words marked school, speech, occupational therapy, play dates, family night, Daddy Night, and other activities. We have used that whiteboard (and since, a conventional calendar) to help our "Sam Man" know what is coming up tomorrow, the next day, and next week. Likewise, sacrament meeting suddenly became manageable when we (mostly Elaine) learned how to help Samuel plan for each stage of the meeting and know how long each part would last.

It was our daughter, Rachel, who realized that we could use these strategies to help make Christmas more successful for Samuel. She suggested that we make checklists for Christmas Eve and Christmas Day to help Samuel know how they would be different and what activities he might look forward to. Together, she and I created checklists on the computer and we reviewed them with Samuel in the week leading up to Christmas. Because one of the items was our Nativity play, Samuel immediately asked what part he would have. Rachel came up with a simple script and practiced with him all day on Christmas Eve. When Christmas Eve finally arrived, everything went like clockwork—and I really mean clockwork, because for Samuel everything needs to be done just as planned!

Perhaps more than anything, our family's tradition of celebrating a modified version of Advent has helped Samuel to understand what Christmas is about and to be excited for it. Because children struggling with ASD

With the help of his sister, Rachel, Samuel has come to better enjoy the Christmas season.

are comforted by rituals and patterns, the idea of regularly getting together, lighting candles, and holding a devotional worked for him. And the repetition of describing what the candles mean helped him learn not only the Advent themes but also gave him a way to visually countdown to Christmas. He learned this so well that the next year, when we were unpacking our Christmas decorations soon after Thanksgiving, Samuel lit up when he saw the wreath and the candlesticks: "Hope, Love, Joy, Peace, Christmas!" he exclaimed. "Where are the purple and pink candles?" The next day, as we got ready for the First Sunday of Advent, Samuel was the first person in the living room. He found our Advent Book and picked the readings for each person to deliver, including one for himself. By Friday and Saturday of each week, he was already talking about the candle that we were going to light that Sunday.

Our custom of having a daily Christmas devotional each day in December has also helped. The year that Samuel was diagnosed, we did not even try to keep him with us for the fifteen minutes it took to "do Christmas." We let him play on the computer as we read most of the stories with Rachel, calling Samuel to join us at the end just for the scripture and song, although most of the time he was not happy with the singing. The next year, however, knowing that it was a pattern, he stayed for the whole devotional, cuddling with his mother while we read the story, occasionally taking a turn with the scripture, and, much to my joy, singing along with us for each carol, even relatively unfamiliar carols such as "Bring a Torch, Jeanette, Isabella."

Now, more often than not, as each evening in December progresses, Samuel is usually the first one to say, "We need to do Christmas." One night while Elaine and I were at a dinner party, he refused to go to bed before we got home because he did not want to miss our Christmas devotional. We light the Advent candles every night for our devotional, not just on Advent Sundays, and he and Rachel take turns blowing them out and opening the day's pocket in our Advent calendar.

We still need to make adjustments, but we have learned not to give up on many of the things the rest of us enjoyed. We sing every night—we just sing more softly than we used to do. We still make all of our many different Christmas foods, but Elaine also makes little hot dogs and pizzas for Samuel so he can have something he likes. So we do some things differently, but there are now many things that Samuel loves about Christmas. I have mentioned Advent and our daily Christmas devotionals in particular, however, because they have helped Samuel understand and join with us for what I know is the most important part of Christmas: celebrating the birth of our Savior. What started as personally enriching practices for me and Elaine came to be useful teaching devices for Rachel. Now, they have become central and reassuring rituals for Samuel, helping him prepare for Christmas in more ways than I could have ever expected. However, they have also helped us all concentrate on the purpose and the hoped-for results of our Christmastime traditions.

Christmas is once again a happy time in our home. In fact, it is happier than ever because of the whole-hearted, pure joy that Samuel has developed for the season. We have at last realized what may seem like a simple dream for many families: every night in December our family sits together, reading the scriptures, singing, and praying together. As I hear my wife's pleasing alto, my daughter's sweet soprano, and now, at long last, my son's precious voice singing carols of the heart, I, perhaps the most experienced singer in the family, can often barely utter a note as my throat tightens with emotion and my eyes fill with tears of joy. As we celebrate the birth of our Lord together, the Spirit is not only filling my home, it is reaching my precious son in ways that I pray will make an indelible mark on his memory and soul. ❖

NOTES

INTRODUCTION: CELEBRATING CHRISTMAS

1. Monson, "What Is Christmas?" 2.
2. Hinckley, "Wondrous and True Story of Christmas," 5.
3. Huntsman, *God So Loved the World,* 121.
4. See Kelly, *Origins of Christmas,* 33–49.
5. See Patrick, "Origen's Commentary on the Book of Matthew," 428–29.
6. Bowler, "Paganism and Christmas," in *World Encyclopedia of Christmas,* 170; Kelly, *Origins of Christmas,* 55–75.
7. Forbes, *Christmas: A Candid History,* 3–13; Kelly, *Feast of Christmas,* 37–38.
8. Bowler, "Opposition to Christmas," in *World Encyclopedia of Christmas,* 167; Kelly, *Feast of Christmas,* 75–78; Forbes, *Christmas: A Candid History,* 45–66; Nissenbaum, *Battle for Christmas,* 3–48.
9. Callow, *Dickens' Christmas,* 114–57; Kalman and Bedell, *Victorian Christmas,* 4–28.
10. Kelly, *Origins of Christmas,* 132; Forbes, *Christmas: A Candid History,* 111–135.
11. Hall, "April 6," in *Encyclopedia of Mormonism,* 1:61–62; Talmage, *Jesus the Christ,* 98. Chadwick, "Dating the Birth of Jesus Christ," 6–11, lays out the considerable variety there actually has been over the years among LDS authorities and writers in treating the dating of Christ's birth. Though somewhat revisionist, Chadwick's subsequent reevaluation of the issue brings much important evidence to the discussion.
12. Bowler, "Dating Christmas," in *World Encyclopedia of Christmas,* 56–57; Kelly, *Origins of Christmas,* 57–71; Forbes, *Christmas: A Candid History,* 17–41.
13. Durrant, "Don't Forget the Star," 42.
14. Whelchel's *The Adventure of Christmas: Helping Children Find Jesus in Our Holiday Traditions* is a delightful book to help children prepare for Christmas and understand the symbolism of its many decorations and traditions.
15. See especially Willes, *Christmas with the Prophets,* 160–61, for her discussion on how President Hinckley's efforts transformed the First Presidency Christmas Devotional into the Churchwide event it is today.
16. Brown, *Birth of the Messiah;* Vermes, *Nativity;* Horsely, *Liberation of Christmas;* Borg and Crossan, *First Christmas.*
17. Millet, "Birth and Childhood," 140–159; McConkie, *Witnesses of the Birth of Christ;* Gaskill, *Nativity.*
18. Schiller, *Iconography of Christian Art,* 58–124.
19. Huntsman, "Glad Tidings of Great Joy," 52–57.
20. Huntsman, "Glad Tidings of Great Joy," 57.
21. Keyte and Parrott, eds., *New Oxford Book of Carols,* xii; Bowler, "Carol," in *World Encyclopedia of Christmas,* 37; Clancy, *Sacred Christmas Music,* 36–37.
22. Prudentius Clemens, *Hymns of Prudentius,* 52.
23. Keyte and Parrott, eds., *New Oxford Book of Carols,* xviii–xxii; Bowler, "Carol," in *World Encyclopedia of Christmas,* 37–38; Clancy, *Sacred Christmas Music,* 22–25, 40–46.
24. Huntsman, *God So Loved the World.*

CELEBRATING ADVENT

1. Bowler, "Advent," in *World Encyclopedia of Christmas,* 2–3; Whelchel, *Adventure of* Christmas, 6–7; Stillwell, ed., *Family Advent,* 6–7, 23, 29–30; Richardson, *Uncluttered Heart,* 11–14; Kelly, *Feast of Christmas,* 21–22, 34.
2. Uchtdorf, First Presidency Christmas Devotional, December 2008.
3. Bowler, "Advent Wreath," in *World Encyclopedia of Christmas,* 3; Stillwell, *Family Advent,* 6–7, 15, 53. For more traditional Advent scriptures and readings, see, for example, Brandt, *We Light the Candles.*

CHAPTER 1: SON OF DAVID

1. See Huntsman, "Glad Tidings of Great Joy," 52–57.
2. Huntsman, "Glad Tidings of Great Joy," 52.

3. See also Gaskill, *Nativity,* 3–8.

4. See Brown, *Birth of the Messiah,* 64–66, and *A Coming Christ in Advent,* 17–18.

5. Ogden and Skinner, *Verse by Verse,* 31.

6. See the extensive discussions of Brown, *Birth of the Messiah,* 57–84; Vermes, *Nativity,* 18–28; Borg and Crossan, *First Christmas,* 81–93.

7. Holzapfel, Huntsman, and Wayment, *World of the New Testament,* 65.

8. See the possible symbolism of the women in Jesus' genealogy discussed in this chapter and of the Magi in Matthew 2:1–12 treated in Chapter 4: King of Israel. Other references include Jesus' prophecy in Matthew 8:11 and the centurion's testimony that Jesus is the Son of God in Matthew 27:54. See also the discussion of Brown, *Birth of the Messiah,* 47, 67–68, 72–74.

9. Clancy, *Sacred Christmas Music,* 60–61.

10. Borg and Crossan, *First Christmas,* 132–36.

11. Brown, *Birth of the Messiah,* 134.

12. Brown, *Birth of the Messiah,* 74–84; Nolland, *Gospel of Matthew,* 86–87; Ogden and Skinner, *Verse by Verse,* 32–33, who also note that fourteen is double seven, the number of completeness. According to *gematria,* or the system of assigning numbers to letters, the Hebrew name *David,* without vowel points, is *Dvd.* The number fourteen is then arrived at according to these values: *daleth* (4) + *vav* (6) + *daleth* (4) = 14.

13. Brown, *Birth of the Messiah,* 74–84; Borg and Crossan, *First Christmas,* 87–88.

14. McConkie, *Mortal Messiah,* 1:316; Gaskill, *Nativity,* 24–25.

15. Holzapfel, Huntsman, and Wayment, *World of the New Testament,* 112–13.

16. Brown, *Birth of the Messiah,* 84–94; Vermes, *Nativity,* 28–38; Borg and Crossan, *First Christmas,* 82–87.

17. Brown, *A Coming Christ in Advent,* 19–23.

18. Cundick, *The Redeemer,* 104–12.

19. Brown, *Birth of the Messiah,* 71–74; *A Coming Christ in Advent,* 23–24; Nolland, *Gospel of Matthew,* 73–78; Vermes, *Nativity,* 21–23; Borg and Crossan, *First Christmas,* 88–93.

20. Bauer, "*tektōn,*" *Greek-English Lexicon,* 809.

21. Murphy-O'Connor, *Holy Land,* 426–27.

22. Murphy-O'Connor, *Holy Land,* 427.

23. While it is not at all clear that the genealogy in Luke is that of Jesus through Mary, Paul had suggested that Jesus was "the seed of David according to the flesh" (Romans 1:3), which was only through Mary (Galatians 4:4); see Brown, *Mary and Elisabeth,* 38–39. For the proposition that Joseph and Mary were, in fact, relatives, see Talmage, *Jesus the Christ,* 85–86, 89.

24. Brown, *Birth of the Messiah,* 123–24; Brown, *Mary and Elisabeth,* 42–43; Vermes, *Nativity,* 56–57.

25. McConkie, *Birth of Christ,* 32–33.

26. Gaskill, *Nativity,* 21–22, 141nn8–10; Ogden and Skinner, *Verse by Verse,* 41–43.

27. Brown, *Birth of the Messiah,* 124–26, 128; Gaskill, *Nativity,* 21–24.

28. Brown, *Birth of the Messiah,* 96–104; Nolland, *Gospel of Matthew,* 23–24, 99n66.

29. See the discussion of Brown, *Birth of the Messiah,* 143–55. As noted by Brown, this particular formula quotation, where Matthew seems to have provided his own Greek translation of a version of the Hebrew original, reveals a number of things about Matthew's use of earlier texts. In addition to his use of *parthenos* for *'almâ,* he uses a different expression than the Septuagint for "shall be with a child" and writes "they shall call his name" rather than "she shall call" (as the Masoretic text of the Hebrew does) or "you shall call" (as does the Septuagint).

30. Keyte and Parrott, eds., *New Oxford Book of Carols,* 178–83.

31. "Joseph Dearest, Joseph Mine," in *Sing, Choirs of Angels,* 11.

32. Huntsman, *God So Loved the World,* 118–19.

33. Ephrem, *Ephrem the Syrian: Hymns,* 78–79.

34. Brown, *Birth of the Messiah,* 132, 139. See, however, the contrary position of Vermes, *Nativity,* 63–64.

THE ADVENT THEME OF HOPE

1. Keyte and Parrott, eds., *New Oxford Book of Carols,* 45; Clancy, *Sacred Christmas Music,* 96–101.

2. Bowler, "O Come, O Come, Emmanuel," in *World Encyclopedia of Christmas,* 161–62.

CHAPTER 2: PROMISED SAVIOR

1. Huntsman, "Glad Tidings of Great Joy," 54.

2. In this instance, Jesus speaks of the blood of martyrs

from Abel until "Zacharias," or Zechariah. If this was Zechariah of 2 Chronicles 24:20 (the name Barachias being a scribal error), he may have been speaking of all the martyrs of the Old Testament, because Abel is the first to be killed in Genesis and this Zechariah was the last righteous man to be killed in 2 Chronicles, which is the last book in the order of the Hebrew Bible. See Brown, *Mary and Elisabeth,* 94.

3. The story is from the *Protoevangelium of James* 23–24, which claims that when Herod was massacring the infants of Bethlehem, he also sought to kill the baby John the Baptist. Zacharias had hidden his son and Elisabeth in the desert, and when he would not reveal their whereabouts to Herod, the wicked king had him murdered as he served in the temple. Because this story also appears in the *Teachings of the Prophet Joseph Smith,* 261, many assume that the Prophet corroborated the story. It appears, however, that the story first appeared in a Nauvoo editorial when the Prophet himself was in exile and may well have been written by someone else. See Brown, *Mary and Elisabeth,* 94–95, and Ogden and Skinner, *Verse by Verse,* 501–2.

4. Bowler, "Christmas Oratorio," in *World Encyclopedia of Christmas,* 49; Clancy, *Sacred Christmas Music,* 44–45.

5. Holzapfel, Huntsman, and Wayment, *World of the New Testament,* 40.

6. Brown, *Birth of the Messiah,* 258; McConkie, *Witness of the Birth of Christ,* 25.

7. See *Teachings of the Prophet Joseph Smith,* 319.

8. Reid, *Choosing the Better Part?* 58–59.

9. Brown, *Birth of the Messiah,* 268–69; Brown, *Mary and Elisabeth,* 25; Olson, *Women of the Old Testament,* 135.

10. Marshall, *Gospel of Luke,* 53–54; Brown, *Birth of the Messiah,* 259–60.

11. Tannehill, *Luke,* 44–45.

12. McConkie, *Birth of Christ,* 25.

13. Tannehill, *Luke,* 43–44; Hornick and Parsons, *Illuminating Luke,* 30–31.

14. Brown, *Birth of the Messiah,* 262.

15. Tannehill, *Luke,* 46, notes that while Zacharias's and Mary's responses were not all that different, as a priest and one well-versed in the traditions of Israel, Zacharias should have responded differently. For the more nuanced analysis I have followed here, see Brown, *Mary and Elisabeth,* 22.

16. Reid, *Choosing the Better Part,* 58.

17. McConkie, *Mortal Messiah,* 1:223; Brown, *Mary and Elisabeth,* 32, 41–42.

18. In fact, the apocryphal *Protoevangelium of James* 10–11 says that Mary was chosen to spin the veil of the temple and that she was spinning the veil during the Annunciation.

19. See, for instance, the discussions of Gines, "Preceding Allegory," 104–5; and Hornick and Parsons, *Illuminating Luke,* 41–51.

20. Murphy-O'Connor, *Holy Land,* 423.

21. See Josephus, *Antiquities of the Jews* 13.9.1 §257, in *New Complete Works*; Holzapfel, Huntsman, and Wayment, *World of the New Testament,* 16, 23; and especially Brown, *Mary and Elisabeth,* 37–38.

22. Barnett, *Rise of Early Christianity,* 92–94.

23. Brown, *Introduction to the New Testament,* 227–28.

24. Marshall, *Gospel of Luke,* 46–47, 51.

25. Reid, *Choosing the Better Part,* 2–3, 55, 57.

26. Brown, *Mary and Elisabeth,* 25–26.

27. Huntsman, "Glad Tidings of Great Joy," 56.

28. Reid, *Choosing the Better Part,* 65.

29. Olson, *Women of the Old Testament,* 84, 98–99.

30. Holzapfel, Huntsman, and Wayment, *World of the New Testament,* 136.

31. Murphy-O'Connor, *Holy Land,* 425–26.

32. Brown, *Birth of the Messiah,* 289–90.

33. Marshall, *Gospel of Luke,* 70–71.

34. Tannehill, *Luke,* 49–50.

35. Williams, ed., *Teachings of Harold B. Lee,* 14.

36. Murphy-O'Connor, *Holy Land,* 169–71.

37. Clancy, *Sacred Christmas Music,* 74–76.

38. Brown, *Mary and Elisabeth,* 28–29.

39. Tannehill, *Luke,* 53.

40. Olson, *Women of the Old Testament,* 139–43.

41. Reid, *Choosing the Better Part,* 75–76.

42. Tannehill, *Luke,* 57.

43. Brown, *Birth of the Messiah,* 346–55; Reid, *Choosing the Better Part,* 75; Vermes, *Nativity,* 137–38.

44. Tannehill, *Luke,* 58–61.

45. Keyte and Parrott, eds., *New Oxford Book of Carols,* 222.

46. Keyte and Parrott, eds., *New Oxford Book of Carols,* 222.; Bowler, "Lo, How a Rose E'er Blooming," in *World Encyclopedia of Christmas,* 134.

47. Bowler, "Lo, How a Rose E'er Blooming," in *World Encyclopedia of Christmas,* 134.

The Advent Theme of Love

1. Bowler, "O Come, All Ye Faithful," in *World Encyclopedia of Christmas,* 161.

2. Bowler, "O Holy Night," in *World Encyclopedia of Christmas,* 162.

Chapter 3: Babe of Bethlehem

1. Huntsman, "Glad Tidings of Great Joy," 54.

2. Holzapfel, Huntsman, and Wayment, *World of the New Testament,* 35.

3. Brown, *Birth of the Messiah,* 415–16.

4. Marshall, *Gospel of Luke,* 98–104; Wallace, *Greek Grammar beyond the Basics,* 304–5; Brown, *Birth of the Messiah,* 395–96, 547–55; Vermes, *Nativity,* 81–87.

5. Marshall, *Luke: Historian and Theologian,* 69n5.

6. Holzapfel, Huntsman, and Wayment, *World of the New Testament,* 36.

7. Brown, *Birth of the Messiah,* 396.

8. Clancy, *Sacred Christmas Music,* 84–85.

9. Brown, *Birth of the Messiah,* 548; *contra* Farrar, *The Life of Christ,* 4, who repeated an earlier assumption, based on little more than the text of Luke itself, that "in deference to Jewish prejudices . . . [the census] was not carried out in the ordinary Roman manner, at each person's place of residence, but according to Jewish custom, at the town to which their family originally belonged."

10. Brown, *Mary and Elisabeth,* 38–39.

11. Brown, *Birth of the Messiah,* 416.

12. See the discussion of Ogden and Skinner, *Verse by Verse,* 51–53, where they also describe personally walking the two different routes.

13. McConkie, *Birth of Christ,* 70.

14. Bauer, *"katalyma," Greek-English Lexicon,* 521. See also Carlson, "Accommodations of Joseph and Mary," 326–42.

15. Kelly, *Origins of Christmas,* 54.

16. McConkie and Ostler, *Revelations of the Restoration,* 155.

17. Seely, "Chronology, Book of Mormon," in Largey, ed., *Book of Mormon Reference Companion,* 196, 198–99; Holzapfel, Huntsman, and Wayment, *World of the New Testament,* 112.

18. Brown, *Birth of the Messiah,* 399–400.

19. Murphy-O'Connor, *Holy Land,* 230; Huntsman, "Glad Tidings of Great Joy," 56.

20. Nelson, *Wise Men and Women,* 7.

21. Murphy-O'Connor, *Holy Land,* 230–32.

22. Holland, *Shepherds, Why This Jubilee?* 5.

23. Porter, "A Child is Born," 3: "The innkeeper has come down in history with somewhat of a notorious reputation. Yet given the crowding that took place throughout the region of Jerusalem at Passover, we can hardly blame him for having no room to offer the couple from Nazareth. . . .

". . . Whether courtyard, cave, or other refuge, the place of Christ's birth among the animals did have one conspicuous advantage over the crowded interior of the inn: here at least was to be found peace and privacy. *In this sense, the offering of the stable was a blessing, allowing the most sacred birth in human history to take place in reverent solitude*" (emphasis added).

24. Keyte and Parrott, eds., *New Oxford Book of Carols,* 361.

25. Bowler, "Away in a Manger," in *World Encyclopeda of Christmas,* 14.

26. Brown, *Birth of the Messiah,* 399; Gaskill, *Nativity,* 85–88.

27. Gaskill, *Nativity,* 89–90.

28. Murphy-O'Connor, *Holy Land,* 476–78.

29. Gaskill, *Nativity,* 90.

30. Brown, *Birth of the Messiah,* 420.

31. Brown, *Birth of the Messiah,* 421; Gaskill, *Nativity,* 91–92.

32. Brown, *Birth of the Messiah,* 129, 402.

33. Luke, in fact, uses the title "Lord" for Jesus fourteen times, more often than Matthew and Mark, who use the title for Jesus one time each. See Brown, *Birth of the Messiah,* 402–3.

34. Bowler, "Angels, from the Realms of Glory," in *World Encyclopedia of Christmas,* 8.

35. Keyte and Parrott, eds., *New Oxford Book of Carols,* 351, 638.

36. Metzger, *Textual Commentary,* 133.

37. Marshall, *Gospel of Luke,* 111–12; Brown, *Birth of the Messiah,* 403–5.

38. Gaskill, *Nativity,* 97.

39. Brown, *Birth of the Messiah,* 427.

40. Brown, *Birth of the Messiah,* 428.

41. Bauer, *"gnōrizō," Greek-English Lexicon,* 203.

42. Brown, *Birth of the Messiah,* 428.

43. Howard, *Spirit of the Season.*

44. Howard, *Spirit of the Season.*

45. Cannon, *Mary's Child,* 6.

46. McConkie, *Birth of Christ,* 82.

47. Gaskill, *Nativity,* 100–101.

48. Brown, *Birth of the Messiah,* 431.

49. See Ogden and Skinner, *Verse by Verse,* 59.

50. Bowler, "Crèche," in *World Encyclopedia of Christmas,* 53–54.

51. Gaskill, *Nativity,* 103–4.

52. Brown, *Birth of the Messiah,* 449–50; Olson, *Women of the Old Testament,* 138–39.

53. Brand, *Observations on Popular Antiquities,* 1:21–29.

54. Brown, *Birth of the Messiah,* 437–38; Gaskill, *Nativity,* 106–7.

55. Bauer, *"paraklēsis," Greek-English Lexicon,* 766.

56. Brown, *Birth of the Messiah,* 438.

57. Brown, *Birth of the Messiah,* 458.

58. McConkie, *Birth of* Christ, 89–90; Gaskill, *Nativity,* 108. For other interpretations of Luke 2:35, see Brown, *Birth of the Messiah,* 462–66.

59. Holland, *Shepherds, Why This Jubilee?* 57.

60. Ogden and Skinner, *Verse by Verse,* 60. For a discussion of biblical prophetesses, see Olson, *Women of the Old Testament,* 83–85.

61. Brown, *Birth of the Messiah,* 442.

The Advent Theme of Joy

1. Keyte and Parrott, eds., *New Oxford Book of Carols,* 273–74.

2. Bowler, "Joy to the World," in *World Encyclopedia of Christmas,* 124.

3. Davidson, *Our Latter-day Hymns,* 234.

4. Clancy, *Sacred Christmas Music,* 77–78.

5. Bowler, "The Holly and The Ivy," in *World Encyclopedia of Christmas,* 105–6.

Chapter 4: King of Israel

1. Bauer, *"magos," Greek-English Lexicon,* 608–9. Brown, *Birth of the Messiah,* 167–68; Nolland, *Gospel of Matthew,* 108–9.

2. McConkie, *Mortal Messiah,* 1:358; Millet, "Birth and Childhood," 149; Gaskill, *Nativity,* 34–35. Ogden and Skinner, *Verse by Verse,* 61, are more guarded, but Joseph McConkie, *Birth of Christ,* 94–96, is perhaps the strongest on this point: "It is of prophets of God [that we speak]! Men who held the Melchizedek Priesthood, knew the spirit of revelation, had studied holy writ, conversed with angels, dreamed dreams, and prophesied as did their counterparts among the Nephites. . . .

   "These special witnesses of the birth of Christ did not come to satisfy their own longings, as did Simeon; they came as representatives of their nations—parts of scattered Israel."

3. Britten, *Ceremony of Carols,* iii; see also Mullenger, program notes, *Britten: A Ceremony of Carols, Op. 28.*

4. Britten, *Ceremony of Carols,* 29–36.

5. When *anatolē* is used for a cardinal direction, it usually appears without the definite article (see Blass, Debrunner, and Funk, *A Greek Grammar,* §253.5, 133). Because *anatolē* originally means *rising* (and hence *east* because the sun and stars arose in that direction), in this passage the Wise Men may have meant that they saw the star when it first arose or appeared. See Brown, *Birth of the Messiah,* 173; Nolland, *Gospel of Matthew,* 109–10; Molnar, *Legacy of the Magi,* 87.

6. Brown, *Birth of the Messiah,* 171–73; Mark Kidger, *Star of Bethlehem,* 73–165; Molnar, *Legacy of the Magi,* 15–31.

7. Kidger, *Star of Bethlehem,* 22–23; Gaskill, *Nativity,* 42.

8. Molnar, *Legacy of the Magi,* 85.

9. Kidger, *Star of Bethlehem,* 253–66, actually concludes that the star, a supernova in March of 5 B.C., was actually the fourth in a series of astronomical signs that began in 7 B.C., each of which had prepared the Magi to look for the nova that others might have missed.

10. Brown, *Birth of the Messiah,* 187–88, 190–96; Nolland, *Gospel of Matthew,* 111; Kidger, *Star of Bethlehem,* 13–16.

11. Borg and Crossan, *First Christmas,* 182.

12. Gaskill, *Nativity,* 43–44.

13. Nolland, *Gospel of Matthew,* 112–13.

14. Bowler, "Lights, Christmas Tree" and "Tree, Christmas," in *World Encyclopedia of Christmas,* 132–33, 226–28.

15. Brown, *Birth of the Messiah,* 197–200; Kidger, *Star of Bethlehem,* 168–70; Kelly, *Origins of Christmas,* 93–95.

16. Kidger, *Star of Bethlehem,* 170–74; Kelly, *Origins of Christmas,* 101–4.

17. This particular formula quotation does not include the standard "and thus it was fulfilled" formula, perhaps because it is in the words of the priests and scribes rather than in Matthew's own voice. Matthew has also either used a version of Micah 5:2 that differs from either the Hebrew or Greek text in several details or altered the wording to fit his purposes. See Brown, *Birth of the Messiah,* 184–87.

18. Wilberg and Warner, "What Shall We Give?"

19. Barrick and Rhode, *Wonder of Christmas,* 12.

20. Hinckley, "Wondrous and True Story of Christmas," 2.

21. Bowler, "Three Kings' Day," in *World Encyclopedia of Christmas,* 223.

22. Bowler, "Father Christmas," "Kringle, Kris," "Nicholas, Saint," and "Santa Claus," in *World Encyclopedia of Christmas,* 81, 129, 155–56, 198–200; Federer, *Santa Claus,* 13–17, 37–43.

23. Cited in Bowler, "Yes, Virginia, There Is a Santa Claus," in *World Encyclopedia of Christmas,* 252.

24. Durrant, "Don't Forget the Star," 45.

25. Ogden and Skinner, *Verse by Verse,* 63; Kidger, *Star of Bethlehem,* 174–75.

26. Nolland, *Gospel of Matthew,* 123.

27. Brown, *Birth of the Messiah,* 114–16.

28. One apparently clear, non-Christian reference to the Massacre of the Innocents is Macrobius, *Saturnalia* 2.4.11, but the emphasis there is on Herod's murder of his own sons, and the text is late enough (early fifth century) that it could, in fact, have been influenced by Matthew 2:16.

29. Brown, *Birth of the Messiah,* 204–5; France, *Gospel of Matthew,* 85.

30. Brown, *Birth of the Messiah,* 205–6; Nolland, *Gospel of Matthew,* 125; Ogden and Skinner, *Verse by Verse,* 64–65.

31. Brown, *Birth of the Messiah,* 206; France, *Gospel of Matthew,* 87.

32. Keyte and Parrott, eds., *New Oxford Book of Carols,* 120.

33. Bowler, "The Coventry Carol," in *World Encyclopedia of Christmas,* 52–53.

34. Brown, *Birth of the Messiah,* 206; France, *Gospel of Matthew,* 90, 126.

35. Holzapfel, Huntsman, and Wayment, *Jesus Christ and the World of the New Testament,* 38.

36. Josephus, *Wars of the Jews,* 2.6.2, §89, and *Antiquities of the Jews,* 17.13.2, §342–44, in *New Complete Works.*

37. Holland, *Shepherds, Why This Jubilee?* 59.

38. Holland, *Shepherds, Why This Jubilee?* 67–68, 71.

39. A fragmentary Dead Sea Scroll version of 1 Samuel 1:22 explicitly says that Samuel "will be a *Nāzîr* forever." See Brown, *Birth of the Messiah,* 210.

40. Brown, *Birth of the Messiah,* 210–13, 213–25; France, *Gospel of Matthew,* 92–95; Holland, *Shepherds, Why This Jubilee?* 128–31.

THE ADVENT THEME OF PEACE

1. Keyte and Parrott, eds., *New Oxford Book of Carols,* 375; Bowler, "It Came upon the Midnight Clear," in *World Encyclopedia of Christmas,* 116; "It Came upon the Midnight Clear," *Hymns,* no. 207.

2. Keyte and Parrott, eds., *New Oxford Book of Carols,* 375.

CHAPTER 5: FURTHER GLAD TIDINGS

1. "New Oratorio Highlights Mormon Festival," 70–71.

2. Cundick, *Redeemer,* v, 7–11, 17–20, 30–43.

3. Huntsman, "Glad Tidings of Great Joy," 52.

4. Huntsman, "Glad Tidings of Great Joy," 57.

5. Packer, "'The Things of My Soul,'" 60–61.

6. McConkie and Millet, *Doctrinal Commentary,* 1:78.

7. McConkie and Millet, *Doctrinal Commentary,* 1:79.

8. McConkie and Millet, *Doctrinal Commentary,* 1:80–81.

9. Huntsman, "'Word Was Made Flesh,'" 53–57.

10. "The Father and the Son," in Clark, *Messages of the First Presidency,* 5:26–34; see also McConkie and Millet, *Doctrinal Commentary,* 2:226–29.

11. McConkie and Millet, *Doctrinal Commentary,* 2:229.

12. McConkie and Millet, *Doctrinal Commentary,* 2:146.

13. McConkie and Millet, *Doctrinal Commentary,* 3:51.

14. See Huntsman, *God So Loved the World,* 116–17.

15. Robertson-Wilson, "Leroy Robertson and the *Oratorio,*" 4–13.

16. Robertson-Wilson, "Leroy Robertson and the *Oratorio,* 11.

17. Robertson-Wilson, "Leroy Robertson and the *Oratorio,* 5.

18. Dayley, "I Come unto My Own," 3.

The Focus of Advent: Salvation

1. Richardson, *Uncluttered Heart*, 15, 71–98.
2. Davidson, *Our Latter-day Hymns*, 229.
3. "Jesus, Once of Humble Birth," *Hymns,* no. 196.

Conclusion: Remembering Christmas

1. Monson, *Christmas Spirit*, 3.
2. Durrant, "Don't Forget the Star," 46, 50–51.
3. Hinckley, "Fear Not to Do Good," 80.
4. Hinckley, "Fear Not to Do Good," 80.
5. Monson, *Christmas Spirit*, 8.

Appendix 1: The Infancy Narratives and the Christmas Story

1. Holzapfel, Huntsman, and Wayment, *World of the New Testament*, 85.
2. Huntsman, *God So Loved the World*, 7, 126–27.
3. Brown, *Birth of the Messiah*, 29–32, and *New Testament Christology*, 105–52.

4. Huntsman, "'Word Was Made Flesh,'" 51, 54–57.
5. Kelly, *Origins of Christmas,* 38–49. For translations and commentaries on the Gospels of James and Thomas, see Hock, *Infancy Gospels.*
6. Brown, *Birth of the Messiah,* 31–32, 48–49, 239–40; Vermes, *Nativity,* 147–48.
7. Borg and Crossan, *First Christmas,* 38–39.
8. Borg and Crossan, *First Christmas,* 41–46.
9. Borg and Crossan, *First Christmas,* 46–52.
10. Brown, *Birth of the Messiah,* 7.
11. Brown, *Birth of the Messiah,* 50–54; Borg and Crossan, *First Christmas,* 4–10; Huntsman, "Glad Tidings of Great Joy," 53–54.
12. Brown, *Birth of the Messiah,* 250–53; Borg and Crossan, *First Christmas,* 10–21; Huntsman, "Glad Tidings of Great Joy," 54–56.

Appendix 2: Preparing for Christmas

1. Huntsman, *God So Loved the World.*

SOURCES

Barnett, Paul. *Jesus and the Rise of Early Christianity: A History of New Testament Times.* Downers Grove, Ill.: InterVarsity Press, 1999.

Barrick, Scott, and Julie Rhode. Program notes, *The Wonder of Christmas.* Audio CD. Salt Lake City: Mormon Tabernacle Choir, 2006. Used by permission.

Bauer, Walter. *A Greek-English Lexicon of the New Testament and Other Early Christian Literature.* Edited by F. Wilbur Gingrich and Frederick W. Danker. Translated by William F. Arndt and F. Wilbur Gingrich. 2d rev. ed. Chicago: University of Chicago, 1979.

Borg, Marcus, and John Dominic Crossan. *The First Christmas: What the Gospels Really Tell about Jesus' Birth.* New York: HarperOne, 2006.

Bowler, Gerry. *The World Encyclopedia of Christmas.* Toronto: McClelland & Stewart, 2000.

Brand, John. *Observations on Popular Antiquities: Chiefly Illustrating Customs, Ceremonies, and Superstitions.* London: Charles Knight & Company, 1841.

Brandt, Catharine. *We Light the Candles: Devotions Related to the Family Use of the Advent Wreath.* Minneapolis, Minn.: Ausburg Fortress, 1976.

Britten, Benjamin. *A Ceremony of Carols.* Edited by Herbert E. Herlitschka. New York: Boosey & Hawkes, 1994.

Brown, Raymond E. *A Coming Christ in Advent.* Collegeville, Minn.: Liturgical Press, 1988.

———. *An Introduction to New Testament Christology.* New York: Paulist Press, 1994.

———. *An Introduction to the New Testament.* New York: Doubleday, 1997.

———. *The Birth of the Messiah.* New updated ed. New York: Doubleday, 1993.

Brown, S. Kent. *Mary and Elisabeth: Noble Daughters of God.* American Fork, Utah: Covenant Communications, 2002.

Callow, Simon. *Dickens' Christmas: A Victorian Celebration.* London: Frances Lincoln, 2003.

Cannon, Elaine. *Mary's Child.* Salt Lake City: Bookcraft, 1997.

Carlson, Stephen C. "The Accommodations of Joseph and Mary in Bethlehem: Κατάλυμα in Luke 2.7." *New Testament Studies* 56, no. 3 (2010): 326–42.

Chadwick, Jeffrey R. "Dating the Birth of Jesus Christ." *BYU Studies* 49, no. 4 (December 2010): 5–38.

Clancy, Ronald M. *Sacred Christmas Music: The Stories behind the Most Beloved Songs of Devotion.* New York: Sterling, 2008.

Clark, James R., ed. *Messages of the First Presidency.* 6 vols. Salt Lake City: Bookcraft, 1965.

Cundick, Robert. *The Redeemer: A Sacred Service of Music.* Unpublished score. N.d.

Davidson, Karen Lynn. *Our Latter-day Hymns: The Stories and the Messages, Revised and Enlarged.* Salt Lake City: Deseret Book, 2009.

Dayley, K. Newell. "I Come unto My Own." Orem, Utah: Jackman Music, 2006.

Durrant, George. "Don't Forget the Star." In *A Touch of Christmas,* 1–51. Provo, Utah: Spring Creek, 2006.

Ephrem. *Ephrem the Syrian: Hymns.* Translated by Kathleen E. McVey. New York: Paulist Press, 1989.

Farrar, Frederic. *The Life of Christ.* New York: E. P. Dutton & Company, 1883.

Federer, William J. *There Really Is a Santa Claus: The History of Saint Nicholas & Christmas Holiday Traditions.* St. Louis: Amerisearch, 2003.

Forbes, Bruce David. *Christmas: A Candid History.* Berkeley: University of California Press, 2007.

France, R. T. *The Gospel of Matthew.* New International Commentary on the New Testament. Grand Rapids, Mich.: Eerdman's, 2007.

Gaskill, Alonzo L. *The Nativitiy.* Salt Lake City: Deseret Book, 2006.

Gines, Catherine Caren. "Preceding Allegory: Byzantine

Images of the Virgin Annunciate Spinning." Art History M.A. thesis, Brigham Young University, 1998.

Hall, John F. "April 6." In *Encyclopedia of Mormonism,* edited by Daniel H. Ludlow, et al. 4 vols. New York: MacMillan, 1992.

Hinckley, Gordon B. "Fear Not to Do Good." *Ensign,* May 1983, 79–81.

———. "The Wondrous and True Story of Christmas." *Ensign,* December 2000, 2–6.

Hock, Ronald F. *The Infancy Gospels of James and Thomas.* Santa Rosa, Calif.: Polebridge, 1995.

Holland, Jeffrey R. *Shepherds, Why This Jubilee?* Salt Lake City: Eagle Gate, 2000.

Holzapfel, Richard Neitzel, Eric D. Huntsman, and Thomas A. Wayment. *Jesus Christ and the World of the New Testament.* Salt Lake City: Deseret Book, 2006.

Hornick, Heidi J., and Mikeal C. Parsons. *Illuminating Luke: The Infancy Narrative in Italian Renaissance Painting.* New York: Trinity Press International, 2003.

Horsely, Richard A. *The Liberation of Christmas.* Eugene, Ore.: Wipf & Stock, 2006.

Howard, Luke. Program notes, *Spirit of the Season.* Audio CD. Salt Lake City: Mormon Tabernacle Choir, 2007.

Huntsman, Eric D. "'And the Word Was Made Flesh': An LDS Exegesis of the Blood and Water Imagery in John." *Studies in the Bible and Antiquity* 1 (2009): 51–65.

———. "Glad Tidings of Great Joy." *Ensign,* December 2010, 52–57.

———. *God So Loved the World: The Final Days of the Savior's Life.* Salt Lake City: Deseret Book, 2011.

Hymns of The Church of Jesus Christ of Latter-day Saints. Salt Lake City: The Church of Jesus Christ of Latter-day Saints, 1985.

Josephus, Flavius. *The New Complete Works of Josephus.* Edited by Paul. L. Maier. Translated by William Whiston. Rev. and exp. ed. Grand Rapids, Mich.: Kregel, 1999.

Kalman, Bobbie, and Barbara Bedell. *Victorian Christmas.* New York: Crabtree, 1997.

Kelly, Joseph F. *The Origins of Christmas.* Collegville, Minn.: Liturgical Press, 2004.

———. *The Feast of Christmas.* Collegeville, Minn.: Liturgical Press, 2010.

Keyte, Hugh, and Andrew Parrott, eds. *The New Oxford Book of Carols.* Corr. ed. Oxford: Oxford University Press, 1994.

Kidger, Mark. *The Star of Bethlehem: An Astronomer's View.* Princeton: Princeton University Press, 1999.

Marshall, I. Howard. *The Gospel of Luke.* The New International Greek Testament Commentary. Grand Rapids, Mich.: Eerdmans, 1978.

———. *Luke: Historian and Theologian.* Grand Rapids, Mich.: Zondervan, 1971.

McConkie, Bruce R. *The Mortal Messiah.* 4 vols. Salt Lake City: Deseret Book, 1979–81.

McConkie, Joseph Fielding. *Witnesses of the Birth of Christ.* Salt Lake City: Bookcraft, 1998.

McConkie, Joseph Fielding, and Craig J. Ostler. *Revelations of the Restoration: A Commentary on the Doctrine and Covenants and Other Modern Revelations.* Salt Lake City: Deseret Book, 2000.

McConkie, Joseph Fielding, and Robert L. Millet. *Doctrinal Commentary on the Book of Mormon.* 4 vols. Salt Lake City: Bookcraft, 1987–92.

Metzger, Bruce. *Textual Commentary on the Greek New Testament.* 3d ed. New York: United Bible Societies, 1971.

Millet, Robert L. "The Birth and Childhood of the Messiah (Matthew 1–2; Luke 1–2)." In *The Gospels,* edited by Kent P. Jackson and Robert L. Millet. Studies in Scripture. 8 vols. Salt Lake City: Deseret Book, 1986.

Molnar, Michael R. *The Star of Bethlehem: The Legacy of the Magi.* New Brunswick, N. J.: Rutgers University Press, 1999.

Monson, Thomas S. "What Is Christmas?" *Ensign,* December 1998, 2–6.

———. *In Search of the Christmas Spirit.* Salt Lake City: Deseret Book, 1977.

Mullenger, Len. *Britten: A Ceremony of Carols,* Op. 28 (1942); at http://www.musicweb-international.com/britten .htm; accessed December 31, 2010.

Murphy-O'Connor, Jerome. *The Holy Land: An Oxford Archaeological Guide.* 5th ed., rev. and exp. Oxford: Oxford University Press, 2008.

Nelson, Russell M. *Wise Men and Women Still Adore Him.* Salt Lake City: Deseret Book, 2010.

"New Oratorio Highlights Mormon Festival of Arts." *Ensign,* March 1978, 70–71.

Nissenbaum, Stephen. *The Battle for Christmas.* New York: Vintage, 1996.

Nolland, John. *The Gospel of Matthew.* New International Greek Testament Commentary. Grand Rapids, Mich.: Eerdmans, 2005.

Ogden, D. Kelly, and Andrew C. Skinner. *Verse by Verse: The Four Gospels.* Salt Lake City: Deseret Book, 2006.

Olson, Camille Fronk. *Women of the Old Testament.* Salt Lake City: Deseret Book, 2009.

Packer, Boyd K. "'The Things of My Soul.'" *Ensign,* May 1986, 59–61.

Patrick, John. "Origen's Commentary on the Gospel of Matthew." In Donaldson, et al., *The Ante-Nicene Fathers,* vol. 9. New York: The Christian Literature Company, 1896.

Porter, Bruce D. "A Child Is Born." *BYU Speeches.* Provo: Brigham Young University, 9 December 2008, 1–6.

Prudentius Clemens, Aurelius. *Hymns of Prudentius.* Translated by David R. Slavitt. Baltimore: The Johns Hopkins University Press, 1996.

Reid, Barbara E. *Choosing the Better Part? Women in the Gospel of Luke.* Collegeville, Minn.: The Liturgical Press, 1996.

Richardson, Beth A. *The Uncluttered Heart: Making Room for God during Advent and Christmas.* Nashville: Upper Room Books, 2009.

Robertson-Wilson, Marian. "Leroy Robertson and the Oratorio from the Book of Mormon: Reminiscences of a Daughter." *Journal of Book of Mormon Studies* 8, no. 2 (1999): 4–13.

Schiller, Gertrud. *Iconography of Christian Art.* Vol. 1. Greenwich, Conn.: New York Graphic Society, 1971.

Seely, David Rolph. "Chronology, Book of Mormon." In *Book of Mormon Reference Companion,* edited by Dennis L. Largey, 196–204. Salt Lake City: Deseret Book, 2003.

Sing, Choirs of Angels. Audio CD. Salt Lake City: Mormon Tabernacle Choir, 2004.

Smith, Joseph. *Teachings of the Prophet Joseph Smith.* Edited by Joseph Fielding Smith. Salt Lake City: Deseret Book, 1938.

Stillwell, Lisa, ed. *A Family Advent.* Nashville: Thomas Nelson, 2009.

Talmage, James E. *Jesus the Christ,* 3d ed. Salt Lake City: Deseret News Press, 1916.

Tannehill, Robert C. *Luke.* Abingdon New Testament Commentaries. Nashville: Abingdon, 1996.

Uchtdorf, Dieter F. Address delivered at First Presidency Christmas Devotional, December 2008. Audio transcript available at http://lds.org/library/display/0,4945,8450-1-4729-1,00.html.

Vermes, Geza. *The Nativity: History and Legend.* New York: Doubleday, 2006.

Wallace, Daniel B. *Greek Grammar beyond the Basics: An Exegetical Syntax of the New Testament.* Grand Rapids, Mich.: Zondervan, 1996.

Whelchel, Lisa. *The Adventure of Christmas: Helping Children Find Jesus in Our Holiday Traditions.* Sisters, Ore.: Multnomah Books, 2004.

Wilberg, Mack, and David Warner. "What Shall We Give to the Babe in the Manger?" Oxford: Oxford University Press, 2001.

Willes, Laura F. *Christmas with the Prophets.* Salt Lake City: Deseret Book, 2010.

Williams, Clyde J., ed. *The Teachings of Harold B. Lee.* Salt Lake City: Deseret Book, 1996.

L'Annonce aux bergers, *by León François Comerre. Courtesy Beaux-arts de Paris.*

INDEX

Page numbers in bold indicate paintings and photographs.